Ace *of*
Spades

Ace *of* Spades

A Memoir

BY

David Matthews

HENRY HOLT AND COMPANY
NEW YORK

Henry Holt and Company, LLC
Publishers since 1866
175 Fifth Avenue
New York, New York 10010
www.henryholt.com

Henry Holt® and ® are registered trademarks of
Henry Holt and Company, LLC.

Distributed in Canada by H. B. Fenn and Company Ltd.

Library of Congress Cataloging-in-Publication Data

Matthews, David
  Ace of spades : a memoir / David Matthews.
     p.   cm.
  ISBN-10: 0-8050-8149-6
  ISBN-13: 978-0-8050-8149-7
     1. Matthews, David, 1967 Nov. 8–   2. Racially mixed people—United
States—Biography.   3. African Americans—Biography.   4. Jews—United
States— Biography.   5. Baltimore (Md.)—Biography.   I. Title.

E184.A1M32 2007
973.040596073052'6092—dc22
[B]   2006043523

Henry Holt books are available for special promotions and premiums.
For details contact: Director, Special Markets.

First Edition 2007

Designed by Meryl Sussman Levavi
Map by Simon Wills, www.simonwills.com
Gun illustrations by David Cole Wheeler

Printed in the United States of America

1 3 5 7 9 10 8 6 4 2

For my father

It seemed unprovoked,
a wilful convulsion of brute nature.

—ROBERT LOUIS STEVENSON, *Weir of Hermiston*

CONTENTS

AUTHOR'S NOTE

This is a true story. While many of the people in *Ace of Spades* are named outright, a few of the names and identifying characteristics contained herein have been changed. To the former, my apologies if my truths are not your own. To the latter, you know who you are.

Ace *of* Spades

CHAPTER I

MOTHER NATURE'S SON

God knows why, labor was induced a month early, on the afternoon of November 8, 1967, while my father, who had received an unruffled phone call from my mother informing him of the impending proceedings, was at work. By the time he arrived at Washington, D.C.'s Sibley Memorial Hospital a few hours later, my prunish skin was settling somewhere closer to Caucasian than Negro. That is what my father, a lean, butterscotch-colored man, was called then—a Negro. It says "Negro" on my birth certificate as well. My mother was white. She was also Jewish.

My father, Ralph Matthews Jr., a prominent black journalist, then forty, married my mother, Robin Kahn, then twenty-seven, in the spring of 1967. They were both working for Sargent Shriver at the Office of Equal Opportunity. Shriver had joked to my father that despite Robin's marked fecundity and the occasion of their marriage (my pop is still hazy about *which* situation arose first, which can only mean that the ghost of a freshly dead rabbit accompanied them to City Hall), "there would be only one raise allocated per household."

My mother was a secretary at the OEO, and my

1

father a public information officer. Back then, whites who worked in the civil rights movement were referred to by blacks as "well-meaning white liberals," a label interchangeable as pejorative or commendation. My mother was obviously one of these *wmwl*, though to her credit, she walked the walk, all the way down the aisle. It seems to me now, under the sickly glow of political correctness, that their pairing was doomed from the beginning. If interracial unions today account for less than 4 percent of all American marriages (by interracial, I mean black and white—the percentages of other combinations is a whopping 12 percent, which suggests that black and white remains the hardest love of all to forgive), then in the heat of the civil rights movement a black and white union could end in rope burns and lead poisoning. With stakes that high, my mother and father must have been in love. Love would have been their ballast in the midst of that squall. None of my father's black friends understood (there's an old Richard Pryor joke that goes something like: *don't ever marry a white woman . . . why should you be happy?*), and my mother's family abandoned her.

On the night of their wedding, my maternal grandfather—who had refused to attend the civil ceremony—called my father to express, in the sincerest of terms, how untenable an alliance between him and his daughter would be. My father said, *I didn't marry you*, and hung up on him. It was my mother and father against the world. That is, until the morning of June 5, 1967.

My father knew very little about his pregnant bride.
He hazily remembers her as an impish, corporeal version
of Modigliani's *Jeanne Hebuterne*. Robin was at once
restive and fey, which lent her the ephemeral air of a doe
stumbled upon in the woods, the snap of a twig or scent in
the wind enough to break the spell. She was in therapy, like
many upper-middle-class Jews of the time, and my father
found her relatively benign quirks and peccadilloes
charming. He was aware that she had moved to D.C. to escape her rigidly Orthodox father (a man, my father recalls,
of some renown in Jewish studies) and he had admired her
willfulness. My father still smiles at the remembrance of
Robin's apostasy, her sly quip that she had given up Orthodox Judaism because there were "too many dishes to
wash."

On that morning, at 7:45 A.M., Israeli Mirage III war-
planes preemptively wiped out the Egyptian air force, and
the Six-Day War began in earnest. The same afternoon, at
a famous D.C. watering hole, my father and some reporter
cronies were tucked into a leather banquette, two or three
martinis into their 80-proof lunch, when in walked my
three months' pregnant mother. In full Israeli army combat fatigues. Fucking *beret* and all. Everything—the organ
grinder, the handlebar-mustachioed waiters—stopped.
My dad's colleagues, always up for a good one, scooted
farther into the booth, elbowing each other with *why
don't you join us* malicious glee. My mother sat down, ex-
changed banal pleasantries, and ordered something to

eat. In what must have been one of the longest lunches in history, the men sat slack-jawed, suppressing titters and disbelief while she picked at a Caesar salad; and no one— not my mother, not my father, not his ribald friends— mentioned the fact that she looked like the Little Drummer Girl. She would settle in to the rest of her abbreviated pregnancy with no further displays; but alas, the bar had been set, and my mother would not rest on her laurels for long.

A few months after my birth, but before Robin left us forever, she did endeavor to have a measure of quality time with me, a "take your son to war" day of sorts. From my father's account of the (mis)adventure, my mother's sanity—to put a fine point on it—had finally shit the bed.

One evening at the office—his belly just beginning to gnaw a telegraph to his brain that perhaps it was getting nigh time for dinner—the phone on my father's desk rang. My mother was on the other end.

I'll be home soon, my father answered, *what's for dinner?* There was a faint echo, his words bouncing back through the receiver.

There was a silence on the other end, which made my father wonder if Robin had heard him. After a beat she replied, *We're at the airport.*

Why are you at Dulles? he asked, the hairs already going horizontal at the back of his tidy Afro.

There was that delay again, and by the time she answered, *We're at Tel Aviv International,* my father knew that something was definitely not right; and a beat later, when he uneasily repeated, *We?* and she answered—her voice and mind four thousand and one million miles away—*I'm with David*, my father knew that something was very, very wrong. I spent a little more than two weeks in Israel, a retroactive Sabra, until my father's exhortations and my failing health shocked her back to lucidity and Washington. No one knows what we did during those weeks; no one but Robin.

A month after my return, in what would become his act of penultimate heroism, my father rescued me from my mother. While a friend distracted Robin at the front door, my dad hurried me (any decent messianic complex begins with the unfledged being spirited away in swaddling clothes) out the back door. From what I hear, it took a few days for Robin to notice we were gone. Within a week she had returned to Jerusalem. My father and I neither saw nor heard from her again.

In addition to the passel of doctors and nurses who surrounded my incubator in the days after my birth, I am told that my maternal grandmother briefly materialized and hovered worriedly nearby. That was as close as I ever got to any other Kahns; Robin and the rest of my Jewish relatives set my father and me adrift in a two-man diaspora, retreating to their brownstones in glass-eyed great cities, or to lime carriage houses in deathless, tony suburbs. My father's letters to Robin's family—in case she ever returned to the United States, us, or sanity—

came back unopened. His sentiment then, and now, was *Fuck them if they don't want us.*

Time heals all wounds, or else infects them.

—•—

Despite Robin's departure, my first memories are of a mother's love. Jan was my father's girlfriend when I was still an infant, a bob-haired University of Maryland graduate student, maybe twenty-two, just gorgeous. I remember her primarily as a name. Any visual memory I have—misty images of bell-bottoms and chunky turtlenecks—comes paired, almost a priori, with a jarring, plaintive, unbidden *shriek*. In that blackest part of the night where the mind cannot distinguish the rumpled pillow in the corner from the world of silent, morphing kobolds, I would strain against the bars of my crib, screaming, *IWANTJANIWANTJANIWANTJANIWANT-JANIWANTJAN* . . . I knew Jan as a need, which is, I suppose, how most infants (if only it stopped there!) know their mothers. Perhaps that is where it—contentment, love—all begins, in the vacuum that develops after a child suckles his fill, his needs met. But that is another story, not my own.

Jan was the first woman to imprint herself upon my consciousness, the way a mother doll made from scraps of carpet and yarn is held fast to an infant chimp's heart. My father was obviously a fan of one-stop shopping—Jan also worked at the OEO, although she and my mother had never crossed paths. I remember trailing behind Jan, my Lilliputian hand in hers, as she went about campus; to this day, holding a woman's hand is an almost unbearably intimate act. I would sit in the back of a classroom, occupied by a book or doll, while she sat beside me, one hand at the ready, even as the other took notes, to brush the hair from my eyes or stick a straw under my lips so that I could slurp the carton of orange juice we shared. Jan was white, and way too young to be saddled with a forty-two-year-old lover and his motherless son. My father was slight of frame, a darker iteration of deputy Barney Fife from TV's *The Andy Griffith Show,* and barely solvent. He has, however, a preternatural ability to make one feel as though there are truths about oneself, and the world, which can be found only at his feet. Anyone who has spent time in his presence inevitably walks away feeling frustrated and unheeded, yet unable to deny his bracing intelligence. To a young girl, possibly laden with white guilt and a slight maternal pang, my father and I must have been irresistible.

We all lived together in a modest apartment in D.C.'s Turkey Thicket Park. I suppose that for my father, part of Jan's appeal had been her willingness to "adopt" me. My father knew nothing about changing diapers, heating Similac, or transporting an infant across the country to cover news events. The first months on our own had been tough, as single fathers were about as plentiful then as Arabs at a Hadassah benefit.

In April of '68, after soundly trouncing Andrew
Young and Ralph Abernathy in a raucous pillow fight,
Martin Luther King Jr. stepped out of room 306 at Memphis's Lorraine Hotel and onto the balcony. He never
made it to his scheduled dinner with Memphis minister
Billy Kyles, and D.C. burned for days afterward. My father held me on the front porch while M60 tanks razed
our front yard, Hueys beating the skies above us. Without Jan running provisions (and this was no mean feat for
a white girl in the middle of a race riot—remember Regi-
nald Denny after the Rodney King verdict? Cube that),
my dad would have had to continue using newspapers as
diapers and catsup as baby formula. After nearly three
years of this, Jan began to explore the world beyond pre-
mature motherhood. The enticements of giving up her
youth, and likely her studies, to raise a child that was not
hers were not enough to keep her around. Jan left me
with those shrieks, and needs, and a plastic Donny Os-
mond toy electric guitar.

While my real mother left me, teats swollen with
rotting milk, Jan had given me a sort of love, as well as a
sort of poison. In some ways, I wished I had never
known a mother's love in any form. Had I never had it,
would I have missed it? The months spent with Jan were
my first hit off the mother pipe, and I would forever
chase that high.

CHAPTER II

I AM A SMALL REPUBLIC

From the mid-1960s until his death in 1999, the rangy, latte-hued D.C. poet/junkie/activist Gaston Neal was my father's best friend. A prepossessing guy, Neal was able to, with no apparent sense of irony, conflate the contradictions of drug dealing, petty larceny, prosody, and black nationalism. He had a gravelly voice, and a serpentine form that, in later years, he would top off with a wide-brimmed fedora, his London Fog overcoat trailing behind him, the whole appearance an almost spectral version of an international arms dealer, or jaded flâneur.

Neal's running buddy—a dark-skinned, slinky hustler named Smitty who was into a little bit of everything, most of them illegal—had a girl named Karen, a flaxen-haired beauty, all Ivory Soap skin and lissome, milk-fed limbs; a Patty Hearst–type white chick who came from the bucolic suburbs of wherever, and emerged from the sixties determined to piss Daddy and America off.

Karen slid into the black revolutionary underground on rails made of Peruvian Flake and Black Tar (drug culture having always been an ersatz desegregation movement, bringing whites and blacks together for the egalitarian

9

cause of copping) and stayed with Smitty until the summer of 1970 or so, when regrettably, if not inevitably, Smitty was slapped in irons and remanded into the custody of the District of Columbia. Karen, who stayed in touch with Neal and my father, averred that Smitty was languishing in a jail cell by dint of his Black Pantherism, and not as the result of various petty larcenies, nor his possession of heroin with intent to distribute (my dad's version of events and likely the truth). The whole minor tragedy was a pitch-perfect rendition of the somewhat recent trend among brothers who, in the face of criminal charges, attempt to exculpate themselves with the following (which, if uttered in your presence, signals unequivocal guilt):

Aww, man, they got me locked up on some bullshit . . . In this instance, "bullshit" does not refer to the specifics of the charges but rather to a set of unfortunate exigent circumstances: the getaway car ran out of gas; the minks and Tiffany china belong to your cousin, but *he's not home right now and he a veteran, got a fucked-up memory so you can't believe a word that nigger say anyway. . . .*

A variant on this theme is the phrase, *got me locked up behind some bullshit* (archaic); however, in both intent and meaning the two are the same. There is no equivalent in the Caucasian criminal world, as whites, generally assured of fairer trials and shorter sentences, simply plead the Fifth, or say their dog told them to do it. In any event, Smitty left his old lady with their four-year-old son Elijah, a wide-eyed boy of burnished caramel.

A succession of babysitters and the sporadic attention paid to me by some of my father's female friends or secretaries had been a piecemeal solution to the new lack of Jan. Karen mentioned to my father one day that she had an upstairs neighbor—an Ethiopian girl—who might be the perfect live-in babysitter. Soon this woman—who had no experience as a child-care provider, but was willing, inexpensive, and, most important, fine—moved into the extra bedroom in our Adelphi, Maryland, apartment. The first night in her new home, she ingratiated herself to my father by eating a cluster of grapes, then convulsively spitting the seeds onto his newly purchased oriental rug. She responded to my father's alarm by cooing, *It will be fine; I love America.* Her reply (between expectorations) to his question, *What's for dinner?* was, *Oh, anything is fine with me.* The next morning, as my father was on his way to work, harried and late (as usual), he watched me toddle, diaper-laden and sagging, below the refrigerator's handle, vainly trying to open it, before falling onto my rear with an explosive *squish.* Cracking the door to my new babysitter's room, he found her just beginning to stir under the covers. With a temperate urgency, he asked her why his son was foraging for food while stewing in his own excrement. She yawned, stretched her arms above her head, rubbed the comforter in loving circles, and purred, *It's just so luxurious,* before rolling over to catch a few more winks.

The next day, after the babysitter had been relieved of her duties, my father asked Karen, *What the hell were you thinking, foisting that woman upon us?* After apologizing profusely, she dutifully proffered, *Why don't you let me give it a try?*

The whole live-in babysitter thing (d)evolved, as these things are wont, into a less than professional relationship; within a few months Karen had gone from paid domestic to plain old domestic. There had been a brief courtship, the walls between their bedrooms delimited by gossamer, the physical proximity of a widowed-by-abandonment father and a similarly unattended mother no match for propriety. She moved her son Elijah (who had been staying with Smitty's parents' in southeast D.C.) into my room, and I now had a brother to go with my new stepmother. He was funny, and from the beginning rather protective of me. His mother, less so on both counts.

Jan had left me, as the reader may recall, with two lasting artifacts of her presence:

> 1) A tremulous need, manifested by the invocation of her name in the middle of the night, as though I had the power of an infant shaman, and through sheer force of will could conjure her to my side,
>
> and
>
> 2) A lustrous, red Donny Osmond guitar.

On Karen's first day as my new "mother" (that word has never issued from my lips; when I see it in print, applied to me, or my life, it might as well be written in Cyrillic) she grabbed my guitar from its perch against the wall and tossed it across the room, breaking the neck from the body. *That's not where toys go*, she enjoined. For a moment before climbing down from my stool (I was at the dining bar, having granola awash in skim milk) I wavered before walking to the broken remains of my beloved Jan. I am sure I cried, but I am equally sure I kept those tears from Karen, because somehow I knew that she did not deserve them; and I believe that I also must have known then, in the cold light of morning, granola putrefying in my bowl, that there would be many, many more tears to come.

We lived then in the Presidential Park Apartments in the suburbs just outside D.C. A complex of three-story apartment buildings sprinkled across small rolling hillocks, fronted by a babbling brook and a wooden footbridge, it looked as though the Lego corporation had been consulted for inspiration. Great adventures could be had on the banks of the creek (at "high tide," which may have been all of a six-inch depth, one could sail a paper boat down its length, or dispatch a G.I. Joe action figure to an aqueous end) or among the branches of the weeping willows and elms. Most of the residents were young marrieds, Jewish professionals, and reformed hippies freshly sold

out and ready to claim their stake in an America they had
grown tired of protesting. There were a handful of blacks,
little boys with ashy elbows and Rodney Allen Rippy
Afros, and little girls with face-distending pigtails drawn
tautly away from their heads. This was the only time in
my life when I was not aware of skin color—whether my
own or that of the world around me. My friends and play-
mates were tiny humans, black, alabaster, ochre, yellow;
it didn't really matter. There are pictures of me from that
time that depict an exceedingly light-skinned elfin boy
huddled among a polychromatic group of his fellows, all
of us beaming, oblivious, a wonderful catnap in King's
dream.

———•———

My new brother, Elijah, had, even at his young age, in-
herited from his father something of the hustler. He was
sly and brash, capable of spinning fantastical tales about
the properties of his favorite T-shirt (which could, in the
most fortuitous of conditions, endow the wearer with the
gift of flight upon his command) or skirmishing with children from the adjacent buildings over the slightest
bagatelles (such as the boundary lines for each building's
play radius). He gravitated toward the older black boys in
the complex, and I was his melanin-deficient tagalong.
While they raced bikes over the protruding lip of the cement path that bisected the great lawn, launching off their
back wheels into the air—two, three, six feet or to the fir-

mament it seemed to me—before landing squarely or crashing violently onto the grass, I watched, awestruck, my clunky motocross-style bike beneath me, hobbled by training wheels. After the "big kids" had gone, wounds attended to and huzzahs offered, Elijah would take me back to the path, and try to teach me how to ride. He took off my training wheels and coached me, little white-knuckled twerp that I was, in the ways of the two-wheeled giants.

While I was, by nature or nurture, a coward, Elijah had the gift of the con man: to take the mark, not for what the con man wants, but what the mark needs. Instructing me not to pedal, just to ride, he pushed me down the gentle incline, and I listened breathlessly as he ran beside me—*don't peddle keep your feet up attaboy you're riding.* I needed the feeling of wind in my face, the summer night and the citric smell of freshly cut grass, outside with my new brother. Karen was inside. Outside was where it was safe.

———•———

A virago, Karen was a fearsome blend of the Germanic tradition of order and efficiency with a take-over-the-student-union-and-off-the-pigs sixties radicalism. She had, through years of congress with Smitty, Neal, and other marginalized inner-city beatniks, become unquestionably *down*, "blacker" in many ways than my father. She was the first in our suburban neighborhood to wear a dashiki. Those loose, brightly colored African garments were all the rage back then, and soon the whole family, at

Karen's urging, was thus outfitted. But no one wore the dashiki the way Karen did—Angela Davis was as Sandy Duncan compared to her. For my part, the tunic's billowy shape made me—a sickly, undernourished manikin—feel as though I were made of pipe cleaners. Only a hypochondriacal, willfully manufactured case of oozing hives spared me more than a few months of Africanism.

Karen had an innate *sprachgefhül*, a hep meets hippie way of speaking; she peppered her speech with that seventies sine qua non noun *motherfucker,* as in, *Look, motherfucker,* which she uttered with a regularity most reserve for *umm*, or *so*. She was a wigger when there was no such word; *nigger-lover* had to suffice. Karen commanded something not unlike fear, even, I think, in my father.

Both incontinent drunks, Karen and my dad's fights were legendary: Thrillas in Manilas, clashes of the titans. Alcohol serves two purposes, to allay or to magnify sadness; the drinker's temperament determines the drug's alchemy. For my father, being high (he is of that generation that referred to drunkenness as being "high" or being "tight") blunted some of the world's pointed edges, those near successes and hesternal failures which, if taken at full strength, can make one—certainly one as acutely aware as my father—sink into listless inertia. Through the rubicund tint of a sherry glass of Harvey's Bristol Cream, my father lubricated himself against the world.

It would be heavy-handed, reductive, but not altogether incorrect to suggest that *the white man* was the world from which my father needed relief. Karen found only rage in that angel's share of her tonic (vodka mixed with fruit juice or, lacking that, more vodka), rage being the actionable form of those sadnesses we cannot name or expiate. Elijah and I would hide in the bedroom during their dinning clashes, emerging in the morning addled and stupefied, each of us like Charlton Heston discovering the battered Statue of Liberty in *Planet of the Apes*. It was as though the apartment had exploded. Couch outside on the lawn, upside down. TV smashed. Butcher's knives lodged deep in the Sheetrock where no doubt one of their crania had been moments before. Their fights did not scare me, inasmuch as I found them . . . *undignified*. What a five-year-old understands about dignity I can't tell you, but I do know that I had a very delicate sense of the rightness of things, which stemmed from an awareness that perhaps our family of two black men (my father and Elijah), a blond, blue-eyed black militant woman (Karen), and me (The Hero), whatever the hell I was supposed to be, was not like other families. Normal families resembled each other more than they differed. They sat down together at the dinner table; joked fondly over peas and mashed potatoes; commiserated warmly over bubbling peach cobbler.

The night Karen made gazpacho, my father stayed late at the office. Elijah and I gathered around the table, as she set down a clear glass bowl brimming with a pulpy, cerise-hued liquid. I was finicky, and my limited five-year-old experience had taught me that soup was, in principle, a hot food. I made a joke about the "Gestapo," about how I didn't want to eat anything named after that organization.

Elijah chirped, *Wow, Mom, what is this?* hoping that an explanation might make this glop less frightening to me. *Karen*, I said, poking a tentative spoon into the sludge, *I don't think I'm hungry.*

Eat it, she said.

Elijah took a heaping spoonful, and smiled encouragement.

I brought the spoon to my lips, and managed one, then two spoonfuls, before vomiting what I had swallowed and the day's previous intake back into my bowl. When I had emptied my stomach, I moved to slide my chair away from the table.

Excuse me? she said.

I thought she was chiding me for being remiss and I amended, *I'm sorry. Excuse me.*

She half smiled. *No, not excuse you. You are not excused.*

I drew my seat back to the table and sat, eyes avoiding the bowl. I listened, nauseated, while she and Elijah slurped contentedly. Once, my eyes betrayed me, and I caught a sideways glance of the tureen stewing under my nose: even now, teeming with bile, the contents looked hardly different than the soup she had first presented.

Eat your dinner.

Elijah's spoon stuttered briefly on the way to his lips. He fixed his gaze into his soup, as though it were Narcissus's pond. I turned to look at Karen. Her eyes—unmoving—locked on me. She had been talking to me. She got up and stood behind me.

Eat.

I may have laughed.

Let me show you how this works, she said. She dipped my spoon into the fetid bowl and brought it to my lips. I began to gag. That was the last straw. She pushed my head into the bowl, where instead of exhaling I puked, and instead of inhaling I sucked in more vomit and squash and tomato, a bilious vicious cycle.

I don't remember what the main course was.

———◆———

Karen soon became pregnant and gave birth to a mewling, impossibly cute boy. We had prepared for his arrival by consulting a book of African names, finally settling on Khari, a moniker that I believe means "king" in some West African dialect. Our little bundle, replete with a diadem of lustrous, ambrosial curls, arrived in the fall of 1972, giving Karen a second channel (Elijah being the first) for her maternal love. She loved in stereo now and I found myself even further outside the frequency response of her emotions. I became an extrinsic member of the family, at least while my father was at work, which was all the time, and was incorporated, as tentatively as frangible egg whites into a soufflé, only in his presence. Quite unfairly, and through no fault of his own, I suppose I hated Khari. Unlike Elijah, he had been born to my father, and possessed the same amount of his genetic material I did. Unlike me, Khari also had the benefit of Ralph-plus-Karen, a mother and father, both of whom he could gaze upon and see his own reflection, the coruscating proof of their love, and his worth, available to him always. This tangible combination was as alien to me as the face of Mars.

◆

When Khari was two, and ready for his first haircut, Karen stripped him, placed a bowl over those cascading locks, and began snipping. I remarked (his naked state requiring *some* comment from a seven-year-old boy, much as nudity, when applied to the *adult* me and the propinquity of a female in said state, would conversely elicit at most a strangled gurgle or a gorked silence), *Oooh, naked.* She passed her cigarette from her clipping hand to her mouth, and with that pained expression smokers exhibit—the half squint as they try to back away from the acrid nicotine delivery device just below their nostrils that after all only inches closer with each breath (they truly are the willfully Mongoloid)—plunged a dinner fork into the bony flesh between my shoulder blades. By this time, we were in a contest of wills, Karen and I, so I did not cry out. I never cried, just as I never avowed pleasure—joy and pain the two barometers I would not entrust to the zephyrs of human interaction. I walked outside and saw my neighbor Toby by the bank of the creek. Toby was the demure son of Polish émigrés, to whom most of the kids, myself occasionally included, were unkind. I knelt next to him and watched for a moment or two as he prepared to jump his Evel Knievel Snake River Rocket across the (three-foot) gorge. The fork stung like an army of fire ants between my shoulders, but I did not let on to Toby, who occasionally snuck furtive glances my way while plotting the coordinates of his jump. I thought the lad overcome with nerves at the prospect of my volunteering as his playmate until, with artless efficiency, he pulled the fork that dangled from the bloody fabric of my shirt and handed it to me. Then we revved that rocket up and sent it flying.

My father, a soft-spoken man caparisoned in a haze of cigarette smoke, his image scored by the bebop that blared continuously from our stereo, was a magical figure to me—when he was home. Karen nodded along while my pop spat short trills into a plastic Yamaha recorder, and Elijah and I held our ears and rolled on the floor in Munchian agony. Sometimes things were not only not so bad but all right. There were black intellectuals in tweed jackets and berets, with exotic-smelling tobaccos and velvety baritones, who smoked and spoke with intensity and great good humor in the caesura between the record's somersaults from A-side to B. My father always encouraged us to stay in the room while the adults dissected the world and its conspiracies (everything with these guys was a conspiracy), and it was there that I learned that if you don't have anything to bring to the table—even well-reasoned bullshit—don't bother sitting down. Among his friends, the jazz dialectics and revolutionary derelicts, my father made me forget about the weekday miseries of my home life.

Karen never beat me in front of my father. She knew that was a line she dared not cross. For my part, I kept the welts along my flanks and the bruises in and around my heart a secret. Unlike many abused children, I would have told anybody who'd listen what had happened to me and who had done it—but they'd have to ask. The only person I confided in was an angel sent to me by my father, as she had sent him to me.

My grandmother Mae lived in Baltimore, and would occasionally visit us in Adelphi. She called me *Davy Wavy*, and was my anodyne—a doting, alabaster black woman who brought not only a reprieve from pain and valises of presents but also scorn. She hated Karen as instinctively as the lion hates the hyena, referring to her as *that woman*, even in front of her face. My grandma was about four-eleven and eighty-six pounds; and Karen was maybe five-ten and a buck thirty, but my granny went toe to toe with her and gave no quarter. Between Grandma's visits, I stored up the accounts of my hurts, doubtlessly enhancing them to the fiction that I was as guiltless as a newborn calf, set upon by a Brothers

Grimm–worthy villainess. Truth be told, by the second or third year, Karen and I had it down to a bloody minuet. Knowing what would set her off, I delighted in my ability to defy, confound, and resist. My grandmother and I huddled conspiratorially together during her visits, my familial odds evened just a bit. Elijah and Khari were fine and good, but I was *hers*, and not a cowlick would be brushed aside without her consent.

By August of 1977, six years since Karen and Elijah had moved in, the apartment had fallen from dishabille to disrepair. When we had company or unexpected visitors, my father would preemptively acquit, *Pardon the mess—we're in the process of moving*, until I very nearly believed it myself. My father had gone off the drink by this time, with no greater motivation than the draining expense of it, and his subsequent clarity removed any illusions he may have held about the state of his battered marriage or his bruised son. He and Karen could no longer be bothered to fight, proving the old axiom that the opposite of love is not hate but indifference. The end came in August. I can recall with specificity the month, because Elvis was newly dead, having just taken his mortal dump. Weeks earlier, before anyone knew about the King's imminent demise, while fiddling with the car radio dial and happening on an Elvis song, I pronounced, *I like him!* Horrified, my father swerved into the gravel shoulder. That is how I know the month was August. That is also how my father knew, though he probably had his suspicions, that I would turn out somewhat differently than he had hoped or imagined.

On this afternoon, I had secretly called my grandmother to tell her about some horror or another when I heard the line go dead. Without turning around, I knew that Karen was behind me, hand on the wall-mounted phone's cradle. I don't remember the phone being taken from my hand, or the snap the Sheetrock must have made as my head was shoved through it. The following day, as I sat on my bed, my father walked in and took a seat next to me. He looked at the split in my forehead, then at the floor. Big feet and little feet next to each other. *You wanna leave?*

Yes, I nodded.

It was that simple, as acts of heroism usually are. I choose to view this moment as a selfless act of love done for me alone, but who knows the miseries he was undergoing or doling out.

While the afternoon sun punched holes in the thunderclouds, and a few fat raindrops cooled the air—*Look,* my father said, *the devil's beating his wife*—we walked out of our suburban D.C. apartment and into my grandmother's tiny one-bedroom in a Baltimore nursing home. My father slept on the pullout sofa; Grandma and I slept in her bed. Motherless once again, but this time—even if I had left my brothers and my friends—it was a relief.

CHAPTER III

TRAGIC MULATTO

Few words were said at my grandmother's gravesite. My father patted the casket, which hung suspended by nylon straps above the yawning hole, the displaced dirt covered by a green plastic tarp, the only splash of color in that frigid, barren outpost. The gravediggers blew into their gloved fists as they hovered near the bulldozer, waiting to get on with it. The priest commended something or somebody, my grandmother most likely, to somebody or something—God most likely—and then we left her out there, alone in the cold. Without turning around, I heard the bulldozer roar-to before the limousine doors closed behind me. I feared that even as we moved farther away, the tableau behind me would expand through the rear window, like the vista in the last moments of an old CinemaScope western, where the mountains, the trees, and the cowboys in their saddles suddenly elongate, fun house–style, signaling the end of the drama.

I summoned every charitable memory (and really, that is all there were after twenty-two years) of Mae from my mind and jammed them into my heart. Every hagiographic image—Mae here now with arms open wide in

25

loving embrace; here again with a chicken pot pie, the fork holes poked evenly across the flaky crust, the steamed perfume of peas and carrots and short dough—had only to do with how my grandmother's death affected me. Grief, like sex and hunger, is selfish. I cursed Mae for living, though I knew grandmas die. They are by definition old. That tautology was not lost on me. I cursed Mae, my father, and myself, for having to "make do" with an obsolete model, a second-hand mother prematurely doomed for the scrap heap.

My paternal grandmother, Mae Jones, was born in Winton, North Carolina, on December 11, 1900. Her mother, my great-grandmother, a domestic, was raped by a white man, most probably her employer, and Mae was the result. Upon Mae's birth she was quickly smuggled from Winton to Newport, Rhode Island—there was simply no way my grandmother's complexion could have been explained away. Mae's foster parents, a light-skinned black couple named the Townsends, owned and operated the Newport Inn. My grandmother learned, from her flinty adoptive parents, how to cook, clean, and pray with an equable, efficient solemnity.

Mae lived in sleepy, chilled Newport until she was about twenty, when she and a few girlfriends moved to Baltimore. I don't know what motivated her—blacks had historically migrated north, and Baltimore was in the other direction, just shy of the Mason-Dixon Line; perhaps these light and bright ladies with their bobbed hair and high school diplomas wanted more from life than watching cod boats chug by, or cleaning ofays' summer homes.

Mae set about finding a job and a place to live immediately upon her arrival. She was a fastidious young lady, and the finest Baltimore accommodation for young colored ladies was rumored to be at stately 1838 Druid Hill Avenue, under the care of Norma and William Marshall. Mr. Marshall was the chief steward of the Gibson Island country club—a posh job for a colored gentleman at that time, and Mrs. Marshall, or *Miz Norma* as she was called (welcome to the South and its fawning antebellum custom of referring to every adult of a certain age and stature by their Christian name; *look away, look away, look away, Dixieland*), was an officious landlady, hawk-like in her devotion to both her two sons and her female charges. Miz Norma made it her first order of duty to see to it that my grandmother was properly launched into black society. Acceptable men queued up, bowlers in hand, outside the sitting room, while Miz Norma offered drop cookies and introductions. My grandmother took her time with these amusements, as she had to attend to the business of finding work.

Until the Second World War, a high school diploma from a northern school was the equivalent of a bachelor's degree from anywhere else. Suitably armed, Mae breezed into the newsroom of the *Baltimore Sun*, showed them her Roosevelt High yearbook and some of her breathless Willa Cather–flavored writings, and was immediately hired as a society reporter—or, in the parlance of the era, a "sob sister"—sharing the floor with, if not necessarily the talents of, one Mr. H. L. Mencken. Soon Mae was flitting about town under her cloche hat, her T-bar shoes clacking along the avenues, in search of sitting-room travesties and aristocratic indelicacies. As fate would have it, my grandmother's career at that daily was short-lived, when she discovered, to her horror, that the *Sun* did not allow blacks on their staff. They had thought she was white. Upon recognizing the error, she walked into her boss's office and promptly resigned. Then, marching three blocks west to the *Baltimore Afro-American*, she became their society page editor.

Back at 1838 Druid Hill Avenue, the extended cotillion proceeded apace. Mae received the earnest businessmen, preachers, strivers, and connivers with neither enthusiasm nor quibble. One ochre young man, however, did catch her attention, as she recognized him, though couldn't quite place him. He was dapper and gregarious, a quidnunc of black vaudeville, whether rattling off details about the wildly popular musical *Shuffle Along* or dishing about his running buddy Eubie Blake (the producer and chief composer of the aforementioned show, the first Broadway production to feature black performers). Miz Norma, full to her gills with Mae's pickiness, swatted her along with, *You mean to tell me you don't rec-ognize Ralph? Ralph Matthews? You work next to him every day—he's the star reporter at the* Afro.

Ralph Matthews and Mae Jones Townsend were married soon after, leaving Miz Norma and Mr. William Marshall to care for their other boarders and their two sons. One of whom, Aubrey Marshall, would go on to be a noted physician; the other, Thurgood, dabbled in the law.

———◆———

The day before Charles "Lucky" Lindbergh touched down at Le Bourget Flying Field on the outskirts of Paris—May 21, 1927—my father, Ralph Matthews Jr., was born. In a ritornello of the Matthews symphony, Ralph Matthews Sr. would soon leave my grandmother to raise their son alone, much as her mother had left her, and sixty-seven years later mine would leave me. Maybe we Matthewses were grotesque, colicky infants, the stink of our baby's breath too much for *two* parents to bear. Or maybe we were living emblems of the disintegration of the black family unit, courtesy of Mr. Charlie. Or, possi-bly, we Matthewses simply chose mates with all the shrewdness of Flaubert's Emma Bovary, moonlight best-ing insight, romance trumping reason. My grandfather was a great man, a good man, and a lousy husband.

Ralph Matthews Sr. was the son of the Reverend Charles Matthews, a Methodist minister, and all the extant memories or documents show the Matthews family beginning in or around Havre De Grace, Maryland, where my great-great-grandfather was a blacksmith, his name either Isaiah or Moses.

The Matthews clan arrived in Baltimore in the early twenties—when they met, my grandfather and grandmother were both recent transplants. Ralph Sr. began at the *Afro* as a reporter, and rose to the rank of managing editor for most of its East Coast branches. He was what was known then as a "race man"; if a person of color did *anything* even remotely noteworthy—whether developing a technique for the first open-heart surgery or getting a cat out of a tree—he was to be held up as an exemplar. I met my grandfather only once, when I was twelve—and that had been to watch him die.

———•———

Mae and my infant father lived with the reverend—my paternal grandfather—at the parish house, 1906 Madison Avenue, on Baltimore's northeast side. Madison Avenue was, at that time, a haven for colored high society, a range of three-story brownstones layered with polished blond oak, accessed by cavernous vestibules, and capped by scrubbed marble steps that lined the corridors of the west side.

Mae worked as a school clerk for the colored school division, while aunts and relatives looked after toddling Ralph Jr. As Ralph neared elementary school age, Mae

and her girlfriend Ivy secured an apartment at the Bellview Manchester, Maryland's prestige address for colored
people, mere blocks away from the parish house on Madison Avenue. The two ladies each had a bedroom—Ralph
shared Mae's—and this makeshift family of single women
and pooled resources shared a cozy common area and
kitchenette. By Ralph's eleventh year, Mae and Ivy (who
was the "private secretary" of Carl Murphy, the publisher
of the *Baltimore Afro-American*) were doing well enough
to rent a full house at 311 Mosher Street (again, right
around the corner from the Bellview Manchester; never a
distance of more than a thousand yards separated these
migrations).

While he was not a regular part of my grandmother's
nor my father's daily life, Ralph Sr. did offer a sporadic
accounting of himself during these years. He was, briefly,
an entertainment editor at the New York bureau of the
Afro (the "bureau," a one-man operation, was likely a
sinecure for my grandfather, who wanted to catch some
shows and live in New York City). My father would on
weekends take the train to visit, his traveler's aid button
affixed to his lapel. He would wait patiently for Ralph
Sr. and his glamorous new wife (Selma, a former dancer
at the Cotton Club who made Josephine Baker look like
Joe Don Baker) to collect him from the Pennsylvania
Station. This remained the rhythm of their relationship
for the rest of their lives: when my father missed his father, or vice versa, one would summon the other for a

visit, whether across the eastern seaboard or across the street.

My grandmother never remarried. By the time I made her acquaintance, she had lived through two heart attacks and a hiatal hernia. A tiny, bowlegged woman, her years hunched over a typewriter (I can still see her at the dinner table, trying to teach me to type on my father's Underwood portable, something about *now is the time for all good men to . . .* then a seamless segue into a bit about *the little brown fox jumped over the . . .*) had bestowed her with an annular hump between her shoulders wide enough to rest a teacup. She had a slight wobble as she walked, from her aforementioned bowlegs, coupled with her not infrequent "dizzy spells."* She never learned to drive and could not take buses on the orders of her internist, who cautioned that the rocking of those behemoths might compromise her already precarious equilibrium.

Though I never had a tangible Jewish mother, I did have—in the zealous, manically hypochondriacal sense— the next best thing. During the eight years I lived with Mae and my father, there were admonitions never to leave the house within an hour of bathing lest I *catch my*

---

*In addition to Mae's dizzy spells, there were ever imminent "palpitations," which required the immediate placement of a sublingual nitroglycerine tablet. I lived in fear that should I fumble in my task of handing her the pills we would all be blown to bits. As far as I had gleaned from spy thrillers, nitroglycerine was highly explosive matériel.

death of cold, and legion proscriptions against everything from eating milk and fish in the same sitting, running about in my "stockinged feet," or straining too hard in the evacuation of my bowels.

Once, in a patent ploy to get out of school, I described to her a pain at the rear of my ankle whenever firm pressure was applied. My grandmother sprang into action, whisking me to the pediatrics emergency room. I described my symptoms to the doctor, pressing the spot at the rear of my foot (which evinced a real grimace, I might add) while the doctor stared impassively. My grandmother, who had the nervous habit of simultaneously twiddling her thumbs and breathing through barely pursed lips, indulged both of these quirks, eyes full of worry for her delicate flower of a grandchild. I was still gesticulating, with woozy theatricality, like Stowe's Little Eva on her deathbed, when the young intern turned on her heel and made for the door, her dismissive *It's your Achilles tendon, bright eyes . . . it's supposed to hurt* with me whenever I venture into a doctor's examining room.

My granny's worries and ministrations were not confined to the medical, but also extended to the social. Once, just after moving in with her at age nine, I witnessed a company of vandals terrorizing the azaleas four stories below her high-rise window. I called out (before ducking below the sight line—in fact, I may have ducked *before* I called out), *Get away from there!*

My grandmother tottered into the room and hissed, *They'll lay for you!*

I left through the service entrance in the basement for weeks afterward. What makes a man.

———•———

While proudly and avowedly "colored," Mae was selectively so. We watched the local television news together, and as the milquetoast anchorman recounted some local atrocity, my grandmother would inch forward in her seat, twiddling her thumbs in anticipation. When the suspect flashed onto the screen—invariably a young black male in shackles, perp-walking toward a waiting paddy wagon or courthouse—my grandmother would cluck, *Would you look at that dahkie?* and shake her head disapprovingly. Her favorite vilification, reserved for only the most deplorable acts against humanity: *Look at that one—as black as the ace of spades.* Just as frequently, and as perplexingly, she would greet the same newscast with a disheartened, *Oh no. It's one of us.* I would sit in front of the TV, scratching my head, trying to figure out how these lost souls could be both wretched *dahkies* and *one of us.* My grandmother's high-yellow caste distinctions were lost on me: black was black . . . wasn't it?

———•———

For as long as I knew her, Mae never spoke of my mother, nor tried to take her place. Perhaps Robin's absence was the reason my grandmother cosseted me. My very presence seemed to engender a sense of melancholy in her, a sighing lament for her son's bad luck and her grandson's maternal abscess. We tragic mulattoes with ghost mothers shared a history of sorts. Her mother discarded her for being too light while, for all I knew, my mother abandoned me for being too dark.

That January day in 1989 at her gravesite, I said good-bye to the only mother I had ever known. My father had lost his mother, the only father he had really ever known.

CHAPTER IV

THE BIRTH OF COOL

With a middling transcript and a stellar college entrance essay, my pop graduated from segregated Freder-
ick Douglass High School in the winter of '45. There was
no "aptitude" test per se; back then the college entrance
boards consisted of a list of essay topics, a ream of paper,
and a pencil. Practically his entire childhood was spent at
the Enoch Pratt Central Library, with no greater aspira-
tion than to crack the spines and inhale the contents of
the Great Books. Thorndike/Dostoyevsky / Mencken /
Whitehurst /Thurber/Woollcott /Faulkner and Matthews
Sr., as filtered through my father's grey matter and
dripped onto the entrance exam, won him a place at
Syracuse University. My father remembers the fury his
high school math teacher, a dark-skinned man with a
lisp, displayed upon his acceptance. *How did thith boy get
into Thyracuth?* he fumed. In an inverse application of the
"brown paper bag test," this same teacher shunned the
light-skinned students in his class under the assumption
that they already had enough of a leg up.* My grand-

---

*It was beyond the pale (no pun intended) for that witless instructor to

36

mother, accompanied by a rousing round of applause, accepted my father's high school diploma for him, my father having already departed for the spring semester at Syracuse.

My father had had almost no exposure to whites until college. There was the laundry delivery man; the corner grocer; and Ralph's erstwhile art teacher, the renowned sculptor Reuben Kramer, who at the time was essentially a shill for the Communist Party, which courted inner-city youths under the pretense of integration via the arts. Among my father and his peers, whites were held in quiet contempt. If, say, a white family in an Airflow DeSoto mistakenly turned onto Madison Avenue—*Boy! Here, now—how do we get to Charles Street?*—to ask directions, well, the football game would be paused deferentially, just long enough for Ralph to dutifully respond, *Yes, sir! To get to Charles Street, you want to—is this a '37 Airflow? I knew it—you want to make a left on McMechen, and keep on going, sir*, which was, beyond peradventure, not the direction to Charles Street at all but the trunk route to Ohio or someplace.

Blacks lived apart in their own city, in a mirrored approximation of white Baltimore. In both cities there was the same stratification based on class: whites were rich

---

have surmised that once these cream-colored brothers and sisters left the strictly limned world of their neighborhoods, they were, one and all—from octoroon to undiluted Hutu—niggers.

Jews/blue-blooded WASPs* (the Colored in black Baltimore); working-class German/Irish/Polish (the Negroes);
or hillbilly-Appalachia-redneck-peckerwoods (the Niggers).

Based on housing patterns, my father recalls, you
knew the value whites placed on blacks: *Long as the help
could get to the white neighborhoods in time to serve breakfast, and those same niggers were gone by sundown, that was
as close to or as far away as white people wanted us to be . . .*

At Syracuse, my dad, like his mother, had been offered opportunities to pass (he was often mistaken for Si-
cilian or Jewish); like his mother before him, he recoiled
in horror at the thought. Even if there were no separate
city for blacks at Syracuse, as there had been in Baltimore, my father would integrate (rather than assimilate)
on his own terms. As one of twenty-nine black students in
a student body of over four thousand, he formed his first
real friendships with whites, many of them rattled war
vets back from Germany, old-young men trying to adjust
to collegiate life with the echoes of Messerschmitts still
ringing in their ears. On my dad's first week at school, in
one of the study parlors he noticed Al Trippo, an Italian-
American bruiser from the Bronx (picture a tougher-
looking Victor Mature), just in on the GI Bill, with his
aquiline nose in a book. Ralph stood behind Trippo, with

---

*I've found that blacks, unlike whites, rarely distinguish between Jews or
gentiles: they scrubbed the floors of Mr. Stevens in Ruxton with the same
fervid strokes they used on Mrs. Epstein's windows in Pikesville.

an eye toward bumming a Chesterfield King, before
Trippo rumbled, without turning around, *Get the fuck
from behind me.*

My dad assumed that racism was alive and well behind
the university's snow-dusted minarets, and that Trippo
had fired the first salvo. But Trippo turned around and in
a fit of penitent recognition sighed, *Sorry, Ralph . . . those
kraut cocksuckers stood behind me every day for six months
beating my name, rank, and serial number out of me.*

After that, Trippo, Morty Gold, Tony Distatio (the
latter two nonveterans), and my pop were hail-fellows-
well-met. My dad found the Italian and Jewish kids to be
the coolest: the former for their cocky braggadocio—the
closest approximation of a young black male's swagger
and verve—the latter for their intellectual curiosity and
almost empathic affinity for the marginalized. Race really didn't matter to these cats. Girls mattered. Bebop
mattered. Cool mattered.

———◆———

When I was a child, my father never spoke of the
mother I never met, save for the terse exhalation, *Bitch
was crazy.* That's the beautiful thing about black
American linguistics: one can dispense with definite arti-
cles, modifiers, even pronouns, and render a life, a love,
my mother's mental illness—a situation as layered as
mille-feuille—into three words as simple, satisfying, and
comforting as a buttermilk biscuit.

As ludicrous as it may seem, I never once broached the subject myself. *Cool*, the gift and curse of the black American experience, was the reason. My dad was, is, and will always be undeniably cool. His cool was as effortless and loose as a Julius Erving three-point shot from outside. The way he and his friends used the word *lady* to describe other men, in the tradition of their fellow be-boppers from the forties and fifties; the way he put that extra dip in his hip and glide in his stride, imbuing a walk to the corner with a slinky lyricism all its own. Cool was how you dealt with shit, how you covered your ass, your bets, and your friends from off the corner, no matter how far from that corner you made it. My pop was the cat who started smoking so he wouldn't have to join the college swim team, because while swimming might have been okay back at podunk colored summer camp Em-lem, at university getting your head wet could *fuck up your finger waves.*

My pop still speaks in a whisper, because cool is, in its way, Victorian. Raised voices and displays of emotion betray a lack of control, and we would not be too far off to supplant the word *cool* with *control*; a people with almost no dominion over their political or economic destiny must fashion what control they can; the control of Jive, a carefully modulated, regulated language, a gatekeeper to a culture, the password changed every few years to keep the barbarians at the gate; the control of that (seeming) chaos known as bebop, the squealing flat-fives, the kick/

snare/kick/snare/high-hat, a maelstrom of recondite ab-
struse blues, the mastery of which requires above all *control* while the air is madness all around you; the control of
the razor pleat of the trousers and the break of the cuff,
though there's no food in the pantry, the mien of looking
good more important than feeling good; cool merely the
condensation from the exertions of control; *oh no, they
can't take that away from—*

Spindly little shit that I was, I knew that by the time
I got to be old enough to ask the question *Where's my
mommy?*—the question wasn't cool. I was hipped enough
to the world around me to recognize in that question a
sense of the clichéd, movie-of-the-week pablum that a
nation of victims spewed. Even at three (or thirty-three)
I knew that if I couldn't keep my mommy, I could at
least keep my cool.

———●———

The cough, which had been preceded by a weeklong
fever, froze the body when it hit, great gobs of phlegm
hacked into bedside handkerchiefs, the green and brown
sputum one day ominously speckled with a single, crimson dot.

Mae took my father to see the family physician over
the Christmas break of his sophomore semester. Ralph
was thin. He had always been thin, but this was different;
his face clung to the recesses and hollows of his bones, the
skin under his eyes purple and translucent. Dr. Ralph

Young (the first colored on staff at Johns Hopkins Hospital) had been the family physician for as long as Ralph had been alive. The doctor came into the surgery, pincenez at the edge of his nose, deep inside the contents of the folder, so much so that Ralph was about to *ahem*, remind him that they were there, the *ahem* erupting into another paroxysm, but the coughing—while bothersome—didn't worry my father nearly as much as the end of the doctor's tawny nose, which held, and then released, a crystalline tear onto the medical chart.

Is he a fighter? Dr. Young asked Mae.

Mae nodded. The doctor forced a smile through dewy eyes at Ralph. *There's only one place you've got a fighting chance.*

Streptomycin was the first effective treatment for tuberculosis. It was made widely available in 1949. My father got sick in 1947. The only treatment at the time was the "rest cure," which was less a cure than a medically supervised roll of the dice. Patients were quarantined and monitored in an adventitious wing of a hospital, where they either outlasted the disease or didn't. Howard University's Freedmen's Hospital was one of the leading hospitals in the country, their sanitarium the best place for a consumptive Negro.

My father approached his recovery with practical determination. His first day there, he asked the doctor, *What do I have to do to get out of here?*

The doctor's reply: *Everything I tell you to.*

Before the doctor left the room, Ralph took a drag off his cigarette (a room full of respiratory patients, all puffing away) and asked, *These okay for me to smoke, Doc?*

To which the doctor replied, *You mind if I bum one?*

The men in that ward—most near my father's age— passed the time convalescing, smoking, eating, and teaching each other dance steps—the good-foot, the huckle-buck, and the lindy-hop—while the doctors weren't looking (but the nurses were). For some, there was no going home. Sheets were silently drawn over ashen faces in the middle of the night, fumigated beds stripped, folded, and shoved into corners.

After watching eight seasons change outside his window, my father left the sanitarium to finish his studies at Morgan State University, a good Negro college in Baltimore, but hardly Syracuse. After living through the white plague, *Siberia* (my pop's nickname for Syracuse) was the last place on earth he wanted to be.

———◆———

After graduating from Morgan near the middle of the century, my father moved to Manhattan, working as a writer for the *Amsterdam News*, *Color Magazine*, and various other Negro periodicals. He was a working writer, which was all he'd ever wanted to be. As his father had told him, spurring young Ralph into a frenzy of the holy trinity of report, write, file—*real writers get a paycheck*. Ralph was in New York way before the Apple had become thoroughly infested with wormy trust fund students and mercantile cenobites. When he wasn't working, he was happy to hang at the Village Vanguard, sweet-talk girls from the Village or Harlem or the Lower East Side— anywhere women and jazz collected under hot lights in the city.

He and his friend James Baldwin held court at the Bravissimo in lower Manhattan, Ralph vying for the ladies while Jimmy separated them from their men. Ralph spent rapt nights at the Five Spot or Minton's Playhouse, watching bebop's first steps, listening to its first words. My dad was a jazz fiend, a monomaniac for the culture. Ask him why, and he'll say that the music *was the only thing happening and everything happening, and if you were about anything, you had to be about jazz.*

While he was working at *Color*, the magazine's ma-jordomo, Dr. F. Havis-Davis, asked if Ralph would mind doing a puff piece on his recalcitrant nephew, an upstart jazz trumpeter in need of some favorable press. Inly, my father was thrilled, but managed to mumble a cool, *Of course.* The interview with Miles never hap-pened, but a friendship with Davis the trumpeter and Davis the avuncular did. Dr. Davis invited Ralph to come share his house, out in the majestic wilds of Long Island, rent-free. Miles would stop by frequently, nose running and on the nod, invariably inquiring after my father, as hoarse and muted as wire brushes against a snare drum, *How much you holdin'?* Miles was always a few dollars shy of copping, but my pop was no soft touch. *I got nothin'*, he would say, patting his pocket and shrugging.

A few years later, when he and one of his latest paramours went to see Miles on Baltimore's famous Pennsylvania Avenue, which hosted every major (or soon to be) black talent of the thirties through the sixties—Redd Foxx, Basie, Richard Pryor, Cab Calloway, James Brown, all regulars on the one-block boulevard—Miles paid him a sort of tribute. Spying him from the stage, Miles waved his trumpet, midsolo, in my father's direction. My father raised his drink as his suitably impressed date snuggled closer. But Miles wasn't done. After the set, he walked to the banquette and motioned for my father to lean closer. Miles rasped, just loud enough for my father's date to hear, despite the pretense of discretion, *Hey Ralph . . . you still pimpin'?*

This was before feminism, before political correctness, and before "Pimp" became a brand name. Miles's indelicacy was an homage to potency from one black man to another, which brings us right back to cool, or control. My pop tipped his drink at Miles, who went off to fix, and my father home to score.

Jazz was an intellectual pursuit, a northern vestibule to the southern civil rights movement.* My father did

---

*Folk music functioned in much the same way for whites, a fact that blacks, grateful for the conscripts, were happy to put up with. My father, unable to tolerate anything outside his sphere of interests, did, in the early

not attend marches or protests, though he would go on to foment and document them. As my father saw it— participation was a compromise of the story. But here's the rub: the story was in service to the movement, for my father, like his own, was wholly uninterested in any story that did not further the cause of black people. His strident dedication was noble, selfless, and important. It also ensured that he would remain moderately broke and unknown for his entire life.

———◆———

During the early sixties, my father wrote a short story and sent it to *Esquire*. An editor there, a matchlessly intelligent Japanese woman, sent him a check for five hundred dollars, along with a note that read: *This is not for the story you submitted; it is for your next story.* He was on his way. Shortly thereafter, James Baldwin's agent signed him and brokered a book deal. My father's wave of good fortune was met by the early crest of the civil rights movement, which swept him along; the short story for *Esquire* went unwritten, and the book, despite the payment of an advance, did no such thing. Instead, my father helped found a newspaper, the *New York Citizen Call*, a weekly meant to compete with the venerable (if somewhat hoary) *Amsterdam News*. Back on the front

---

sixties, cavil at a young folkie molesting a guitar in an empty corner of Café Wha? one afternoon: *Man, cut that racket out.* Thankfully, Bob Dylan kept right on playing.

lines, my father's own chance for fame and literary *renom* had passed.

The *Citizen Call* was staffed by my father, who served as the managing editor, a man named Chuck Stone, who was formerly the editor of the *New York Age* (another New York–based Negro weekly), a receptionist (Marlene Clark, who later went on to appear on TV's *Sanford & Son* as Demond Wilson's—Lamont's—girlfriend), and a young Jewish reporter poached from the *New York Post*. Barely a week into the paper's inception, Ms. Clark rushed into my father's office stammering, *Mr.—um, Ralph, there's a . . . to see you . . . Malcolm X!* Craning his neck out his office door, my father barely repressed a *holy shit.*

All he knew about Minister Malcolm was that he was a fearsome new voice on the Harlem scene. Ralph had read with consternation mainstream media accounts of the Nation of Islam's stand on the deviltry of the white man, and knew that Malcolm was the face of the Nation. This was a world far removed from the middle-class integrationist theories on which my father had been raised. Ralph gave Malcolm a walking tour of the paper's offices, the minister towering over everyone in the room, commenting as he surveyed, *Yes, well, Mr. Matthews, I'm very impressed with your enterprise, looks very professional, the quality of the paper thus far is exemplary . . . however . . .* and said, with a look straight down his black-frame glasses at the nearly palsied Jewish reporter hiding against the mimeo machine, *I have a distinct problem with your hiring practices, my brother.* Malcolm was at once sardonic and completely in earnest. My father loved him almost immediately.

Nothing was done in Harlem without Malcolm's (working under the auspices of the Nation of Islam) knowledge and approval. For the three-year life of the newspaper, my father and Malcolm held weekly, pre-deadline meetings every Friday at the Temple Number Seven Restaurant—Malcolm's de facto business office, right around the corner from the Muslim Mosque Number Seven—to discuss the state of the world, and the state of the paper. Malcolm tried, halfheartedly, to convert Ralph, but all the talk of mother ships and evil scientists was not (my father suspected that even Malcolm took the Nation's creation myths *cum grano salis*) an allurement to a critical thinker like Ralph. (And no way was my pop giving up pork chops, liquor, and women.) At one point Malcolm asked Ralph to edit the NOI's paper of record, *Mohammed Speaks,* an offer my father politely (oh, so politely) refused. Aside from teleological differences, my father found little in Malcolm's philosophies with which to quibble. Ralph may not have believed that the white man was guilty of every crime against the world's darker peoples, but he sure as hell believed the jury was still out. So harmoniously aligned were their sensibilities that, as Malcolm signed autographs in the lobby of Baltimore's Morgan State University in the aftermath of a 1964 debate with Jewish sociology professor Augie Myers, he deflected the throngs of quizzical students with a wave of his pen toward my father: *Talk to Brother Matthews; he knows all the stuff you need to know.*

Ralph saw Malcolm as much as any non-Muslim could during the years of his ascent within the NOI, and though my father had moved back to Baltimore by the time Malcolm split from that organization, they remained in regular contact. My father's most wistful reminiscences of his good friend are bookends of Malcolm's life in public service.

On Floyd Patterson Day, in the summer of 1960, my father was tooling up 125th Street in his new (new to him, at any rate) MGB convertible. Malcolm, standing on the corner, walked over to my father at the light.

This is a very interesting car you have here . . . this is a British car, right? A car of the landed gentry of merry olde England, isn't that right? What—Brother Matthews—are the identity issues of a black man, driving a colonial car, to the celebration of a black warrior, in Harlem—can you put all that together for me, Brother Matthews?

A few days later, my father once again pulled up to a light at 125th Street, a familiar black Chrysler idling next to him. My father honked, and Malcolm looked over. Over the sputter of his MGB my father asked, *Minister Malcolm, what is one of our black nationalist leaders doing—driving a piece of fascist, Detroit junk?*

The light changed, both men shifted into first, and

Malcolm answered, struggling to hold back the edges of a smile, *Trying to get home.*

Relocated to D.C. by this point (and scant months away from meeting my mother), my father called Minister Shabazz (this was after his hajj) on Valentine's Day 1965, worried for his safety after learning that his house had been firebombed that morning. My father asked the minister, who was disconsolate, if he had any theories as to who was behind the attack, and he said, *You've been around us long enough to know, Brother Matthews . . . only a Muslim can get another Muslim.*

Seven days later, on February 21, Minister Malik El Shabazz took the podium at the Audubon Ballroom.

CHAPTER V

BETTER THE DEVIL YOU KNOW

The ride from Adelphi, Maryland, usually took an hour, time I spent woolgathering at the passenger-side window, my chin on my arm, as the landscape atrophied, the coniferous greens and deciduous browns along the D.C. corridor of I-95 turning to smokestacks and steel-yards as Baltimore loomed. On the day we left Adelphi for good, there was little in that industrial scenery to support my fantasies (the elves and fairies, knights and Sasquatches I had conjured there were not easily transplanted into the rusted geometry of Bethlehem Steel), so by around the forty-five-minute mark, I lay prone in the backseat, and watched the sky roll by. Then the car slowed, made a sharp right into the looping driveway, and where there had once been skyline, huge white letters against brick: *The Memorial Gardens Apartments*. We were home, a senior citizens' retirement home, just inside the border of Baltimore's posh Bolton Hill neighborhood.

Karen, my father's recently sloughed wife, had never set foot in my grandmother's sunlit, doilied, one-bedroom apartment, so it had maintained for my nine-year-old self the aura of a sanctuary. There were two rooms—a living room of ten by twelve and a bedroom of perhaps two-thirds that size. The apartment, number 413, overlooked a gorgeous flag of green lawn below, and the rear of the building hid a garden as florid as any since Havilah. Five-foot hedges divorced this half acre of manicured bluegrass, paved elliptical walkways, and tangled rosebushes from all that lay outside its boundaries.

The apartment itself was a wonderland of morbid prophylaxes. The bathroom had strategically placed chrome bars and handrails affixed throughout, to mitigate or rescue residents from the "falls" that seemed to smite the decrepit with hip-shattering regularity. The intercom by the front door had a lever, at mouth level, to which a length of string and a plastic knob had been tied, ensuring that as long as one could crawl, help was but a tug away. In the way that jittery parents attempt to "child-proof" their homes, thus was the Memorial Gardens made, if charily, "death-proof."

The living room housed a pullout couch with a greenish-wool check pattern, as though a kilt had puked; a recliner; and a magnificent, hearthlike TV with a twenty-inch screen—tops—that was encased in enough wood to build a dining room set. This was my ersatz black-and-white parent. Do you know who Noam Pitlik, Randolph Mantooth, or Gregory Sierra are? I do, and scores more of those people with an alacrity most often reserved for family reunions. (I have no excuse for the months and years of my addiction that followed, but there are worse habits, I suppose, like Islam or karaoke). There was little else to do but gorge on TV in those weeks after my father and I moved in with her. I had no friends, nor any means to seek them out. By this point, my father was already at his new job as managing editor of the *Baltimore Afro-American*,* leaving me to retreat even further into a world in which I was fast becoming the sole inhabitant: the planet myopia.

There was, of course, the problem of school. We had arrived in September and, to my delight, there was no immediate mention of my matriculation. Though I had my hopes, I did not for a moment think that I would not return to my studies. While I waited for the other shoe to drop, I had, in addition to the boundless pleasures of television, the funereal dumb-shows GI Joe and I staged in the hot LZ of Grandma's living room. I would fix a length of string from the lip of the kitchen wall divider to the leg of the recliner and rappel Joe (by dint of his "kung-fu grip," which would have been more aptly described as "gnarled rubber that will break off at the slightest use or wear") across the length of the apartment

---

*Which could lead a less chimeric sort to conclude that my father had shored up possibilities for work *before* the rash, impassioned "rescue" of his beaten son; but to the dream that fires the furnace, give all your heart and soul.

in some emprise involving Jerries or Nips,* while Joe (my proxy) usually came to a baroque, sanguinary end, the whole drama (it could last hours) punctuated by a lavish state funeral, (my grandmother's) silk scarves pressed into service as coffin (shoe box) liners, while I stood at attention, a salute (one single tear) as earnest as any young John-John had given to his fallen father. That took me up until three o'clock.

Good television didn't begin until three o'clock, with the advent of UHF channel 45's *Captain Chesapeake*. In those days, local stations had their own programming. *Captain Chesapeake,* the after-school kid's show, was framed around the adventures of a middle-aged ship's captain who one day fell overboard, only to be rescued by a lovable sea monster (a life-size puppet that would have occasioned very little envy in Jim Henson) named Mondy.† His minute-long skits were the interludes in a roster of *The Banana Splits, Scooby-Do, Speed Racer*, and *Gilligan's Island.* "Captain C" taught me my first lessons in identity and truthfulness.

During the mercilessly decontaminated late-night horror feature (*Ghost Host Theatre*) I noticed my beloved Captain Chesapeake, sans skipper's hat, hawking used

---

*The former slang for Nazis, courtesy of *Hogan's Heroes*; the latter slang for Japanese soldiers, courtesy of *McHale's Navy*.

†The Baltimore accent is like no other, and there is little to recommend it. It is phonated with lazy vowels and rounded consonants; to wit, Mondy, the sea monster's name, is pronounced Môen-dē.

cars in a local commercial. I was crestfallen. At the end of his own show, the Captain looked into the camera and admonished his youthful audience to *be somebody important; be yourself*. Captain, I thought, sail thyself. I continued to watch him, but now I could see the poor sap—whoever the vaunted Captain C was—the sour perfume of blended whiskey about him, shuffling from one "acting" gig to another, touting old Buicks or performing at a rich brat's birthday party. I dimly understood that he was doing what he must to survive, and I took from this revelation my own retrofitted valediction: *You can be somebody important, even if the definition of that somebody is negotiable.*

Grandma wanted to send me to a private school, and for weeks after my arrival glossy pamphlets from the McDonogh School, Park, and Friends lay scattered across her coffee table like the real estate leads from *Glengarry Glen Ross*. She likely saw me in a crested blazer, playing a bit of touch football on the rolling green during autumn afternoons, my mornings spent earnestly conjugating Latin with my dashing coevals. What fueled this chimera—aside from her general New Englandish sense of the rightness and legitimacy of institutions—is beyond me. Her income, a social security–pension admixture, was somewhere in the neighborhood of $17,000 per year, which was enough to cover tuition at any one of those academies had we been content to subsist on hog maws and alms. But I was her jewel, and would have nothing but the best. Perhaps she wanted to confer the gift of integration that my father never had upon me. I too could be one the "talentless 90th," with nothing to stop my ascent to the middle except the 2.61 by 6.14–inch greenery by which all men are rendered equal.

Quite correctly, my father noted that weeks spent alone in a room with my grandmother were beginning to solidify my natural tendencies toward the foppish. He would come home evenings to the discomfiting tableau of my grandmother and I embroiled in a heady game of pinochle, *Marcus Welby, M.D.* droning softly in the background. On the ludicrous assumption that even a down payment on the blazer could have been secured, private school would have been the last straw. My father was not going to stand idly by while his heir apparent deliquesced into a shimmering custard. I was going to public school.

To some nine-year-old boys, nothing squares the shoulders or fixes the pride like entree to a new school, that wonderland full of strange, exciting faces and unlimited possibilities.* Like some naïf right out of Kipling, I was led by my grandmother into my new classroom three weeks into the fourth grade. After walking with me the

---

*These jocund, expansive, well-adjusted American children, however, are freaks to me, as inscrutable as a world of John Wayne Gacys or born-again Christians.

four blocks to Mt. Royal Elementary, school number 66, my grandmother deposited me in a chair outside the principal's office. From that perch, I spied her interviewing the principal, a middle-aged black woman named Mrs. Gross. Many smiles and nods passed to and fro, and I suspect that my grandmother, by dint of her long and distinguished career in public education, was being granted a rather elaborate audience by Mrs. Gross. Moments later, the two women escorted me upstairs to Mrs. Eberhard's homeroom class (already in session). I had never felt so completely, utterly, on my own. Mrs. Eberhard, a flaxen-maned woman in her thirties, made an introduction of sorts, and every student turned around to study me. Most of those leery faces, I could not help but notice, were black.

At the end of homeroom, Mrs. Eberhard asked the class if anyone lived in Bolton Hill. There were a few noncommittal mumbles and averted eyes, and after a protracted silence, *Mark*, I heard her say, *you'll be David's buddy today.* And with that, Mark Anderson, a blond, good-natured kid with teeth as straight as his hair, quickly withdrew his raised hand with all the enthusiasm you would expect in one selected for such an assignment. While we filed out of homeroom, he made a game overture, a play date later that afternoon. There, en route to that first day of classes, the son of my father had only a few moments left to live.

In some ways, Baltimore, Maryland, circa 1977, had
changed little from the Baltimore of my father's youth.
There was now a majority black population, a minority
white population (the demographic had reversed after
World War II), and practically no Asians, Hispanics, or
Indians.* Inexorably, the city's neighborhoods were still
unequivocally segregated. The reader may remember
that my grandmother's migration within black Baltimore had been confined to a four- or five-block radius
over the course of forty-odd years. Her post-retirement
address in Bolton Hill, a Waspy enclave of tony brownstones (think of a parochial simulacrum of Manhattan's
Gramercy Park), was mere feet from her previous addresses. Trouble was, her prior historically middle-class,
black neighborhood had turned, in the scant handful of
decades since the war, into a roiling black ghetto. Below
her high-rise window, just beyond the Arcadian lawn in
front and the concealed garden aft, was another world of
housing projects, roaming street gangs, and bleating
squad cars. While such tumult may have been common
in, say, New York City, in Baltimore it was not a mere

*When I say "practically no" the reader will have come, by this time, to
understand my tendencies toward the polemic. I am sure there were
"some," but they were not in evidence in daily life, as scarce as Lipstick
Lesbians.

distraction or the "price of living in the city"—it was danger.

It may be difficult to comprehend the propinquity, the stark contrasts, between Bolton Hill and its environs. This was not merely a case of a black neighborhood abutted against a white one. The residents of Bolton Hill were *rich*, landed blue bloods, who, having watched their surroundings literally darken, nonetheless refused to leave their million-dollar homesteads. They were as insufferable and delusional as Rhodesian colonists sipping shandies on porches in cool linens, unable to accept that independence was nigh, and that the drums would soon stop. They were smug professionals whose children attended the McDonogh, Park, and Friends triumvirate; or liberal martyrs who kept their children in public school (number 66) to make a point. In the five square blocks of this WASP reserve, the brothers and sisters were *poor*, dispossessed, forgotten, and, right outside the dwindling campfires, hungry.

Those proscribed blocks became my DMZ for the next eight years. The city, hitherto simply a haven from the dangers of Karen, now took on a frank menace. Not a place you went to, it was a place you lived through, a lover discovered under harsh daylight or the glare of convenience-store fluorescents. My earliest years in the idylls of suburbia had been spent in color-blind adoration of my black father, my brother Elijah, my ashy friends

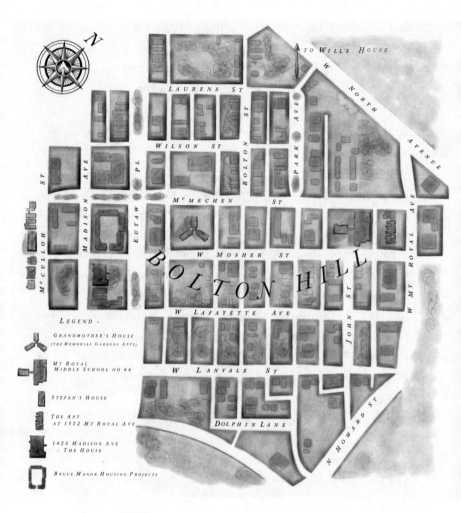

Bolton Hill was essentially the area between Eutaw Place (on the side of the street closest to my grandmother's) to the west; Mt. Royal Avenue to the east; Lanvale Street to the south; and Laurens Street to the north; all else was the ghetto.

with puffy Afros, but now things were different. This was the city, and these were niggers.

———◆———

What are you, hey he won't answer us look at me what are you? the black and white faces herded around me demanded, twenty minutes into my first day at school. I clammed up. No one had ever asked me what I was. In the hallway, in those few moments between homeroom and the start of classes, I immediately grasped that any response on my part could be disastrous. These kids swarming around me, grilling me about my racial identity, seemed emotionally invested—though they knew nothing about me yet—in my answer. I had a hunch—based on their avidity—that to the question: *What are you?* there was a *wrong* answer. Nearly thirty years later, the bullshit response to that bullshit question would be the mawkish rejoinder, *I'm a human being.* But mercifully, political correctness had not yet been borne of the loins of Ivy League white-liberal guilt and offered as an udder on which the disaffected could suckle. So I said nothing, inflaming them with a torturous game of racial keep-away.

Like the bits of the city I had seen while traveling to and around Baltimore (ensconced behind the glass of my father's Mazda sedan) Mt. Royal Middle School, school number 66, had a black population of 85 percent. This was a direct demographic inverse of my previous, wholly

unremarkable school, Adelphi Elementary. Oddly, the
white kids seemed equally fervid in their inquiries. Even
as the old, indeterminate me was dying, something was
being born. Presented with not only the opportunity but
an exigent *need* to choose a racial identity, I froze. Unable
to process the magnitude of what was being asked, only
the urgency impressed itself upon me. I recalled the
misty years of dashikis and bebop, my brothers'—one
burnished and one blond—faces that looked at once like
everyone I had known and loved and yet different from
my own. The choice was both impossible and necessary:
identify myself or have it done for me. In none of the
kids' questions was the implicit, inelastic clause *mixed*.
These children I had just met, and the voice of Captain
Chesapeake, my grandmother's lilting *dahkies*, and *black
as the ace of spades*, and whatever flimsy material I was
made of would become the midwives of my all-American
deformity.

Nonplussed, we walked in a herd, as though I were a
reprobate head of state ambushed by reporters outside a
lurid hotel. Fairly frothing at this point, they were hopping up and down, shouting their own guesses from the
sidelines, a racialist Greek chorus of, *Black! White! You
crazy?! He('s) too light/dark to be black/white!* I think
someone, a class picador, shouted, *Chinese!* Which sent a
palliative belly laugh through the crowd, myself included. My identity became their collective monomania

in those moments, and as both an interloper and a loner, I had to carefully gauge the levels of their frustrations. Had I demurred for too long, ostracism—or school-yard violence for all I knew—would have been their only recourse. It was easy to discern their puzzlement: their world was as insoluble as if their differing races had been made up of either oil or water. There were many shades of black, from indigo to browned butter, but none quite as sallow as my own, and there were variegated white faces, from chalk to flushed crimson, but none quite so thick-lipped, with a nose slightly widened in an equine flare. The power of wonder I held in those hallways—I was a mute Jesus en route to Capernaum—but the Romans would not be held off much longer. As the mob, with me as the cynosure, reached our first-period class, they resorted to a subtler though no less politic tack:

What kind of music [do] you like?

Even though I (marginally) enjoyed the Jackson Five, that admission might provide partisan ammo to the students most consumed with what I was, so in a panic I threw out names of performers my grandmother liked. That's how fucked up racism is. What else on earth could have motivated a young boy, first hour in a new school, to throw away any chance at acceptance—forget about cool, we're talking basic *Lord of the Flies* do-we-eat-this-kid-or-not survival—with this reply: *Beverly Sills*. Peter, the fraternal twin of a chestnut-haired girl who looked just like him, right down to the dappling of freckles, sniggered *Beverly Sills?!* his voice cracking on the "ills." I staved off an almost immediate lynching only by quickly adding the Monkees, the Beatles, the Jackson Five—the J5 tossed in as supernumeraries from which I hoped no official identity on my part could be deduced.

I was David Ralph Matthews. That had been as far a depth as I'd ever needed to plumb. Those first few moments in the hallway had alerted me to the importance they (and, to a larger extent, Baltimore, and even larger extent, America) placed on white or black. Pick *one.* By the time I hit the cafeteria a few hours later, I was in a state of racial hyperesthesia, my eyes pried open to the realities and urgency of my situation.

———◆•◆———

Beatings and all, things were much simpler in Adelphi. All Karen had ever asked me was *How do you like that?* or *Not so funny now, is it?*—infinitely easier questions to answer. My eyes scanned the cafeteria and saw a sea of black faces surrounding an isthmus of white kids. There was little mingling. I did not contemplate the lack of congress, it was a tacit part of the physical geography—an impassible gorge, an unassailable summit—and I was no explorer; I was a weak-kneed outsider, a yellowed freak. Lunch tray in hand, I made a final and (at least I like to tell myself) psychologically logical choice: I joined the tableful of kids who most looked like me. The white kids were my proximate copies: they had the same nasal honk* and nerdy diction; their costumes were the same, shaggy post–Haight-Ashbury moptops, blue jeans, and wide collars. In those incipient hours leading to cafeteria period, I had noticed a loose, breezy, effortless charge that crackled through the black kids, which I knew I didn't possess. They were playing "the dozens," executing ligament-defying disco moves and doing double Dutch out on the playground; they were alive and cool. The only experience I had with cool had been vicarious, watching my father and his friends and feeling their vague sense of disappointment when I couldn't mirror their behavior.

In some way I wasn't yet aware of, urban black people scared me. A fop, a dandy, I found their physicality alarming. Karen's beatings had sent me inside myself, made me a watcher rather than a participant. Watchers could observe human interaction, free from its charms and its dangers, while participants ran the risk of being noticed, and, once noticed, singled out; once singled out, punished. The posturing and braggadocio among the black kids required an outgoing temperament I couldn't

---

*A bit of arcana: the word *honky* comes from the nasal tone Caucasians vocalize with, a result of the longer nasal passages required to warm the Arctic air before it enters the lungs.

muster. I didn't know the one about how *your mama's so dumb she failed her Pap test*; I didn't know that with the wrong intonation, or the wrong addressee, any mention of one's mama would lead to a table-clearing brawl, a claque of kids screaming, *A fight, a fight, a nigger and a white, if the nigger don't win, we all jump in.*

The group of white kids, hunched over their *Starsky & Hutch* lunch boxes and Garbage Pail Kids trading cards, didn't look like they'd be doing any rumbling any-time soon. On that day, in that moment, I came to be-lieve that if I had said I was black, I would have, perforce, to spend my life convincing my own people.

The wind that swept through my house of cards was Mark Anderson, my erstwhile buddy for the day, who looked up from his *Fantastic Four* comic book, caught my eye across the cafeteria, scooched over in his seat, and nodded me in. That was it. By the code of the cafeteria table, which was just as binding in that time and place as the laws of Jim Crow or Soweto, I was white.

<hr />

Being white meant getting over at school 66. The teachers knew they had fallen smack-dab into the middle of a honey pot. They didn't have to learn judo in order to pry knives and zip guns away from their students, the way teachers in those *other schools* did. Mt. Royal Middle School was a coveted-zone school that many whites from beyond the proscribed district finagled—through contrived or fabricated addresses or a sympathetic administrator's blind eye—admittance.*

The black kids at 66 were generally smart and, at least in bearing, not so different from my black friends back in the suburbs, save for their veneer of urban toughness. The teachers, however, coddled the white kids, assuming (probably correctly) that if their parents pulled them out of 66, the school would lose valuable tax revenues and quickly become one of *those schools*. The teachers (black and white) had a brusque, dismissive way of dealing with the black kids, ignoring their raised hands as well as their insolent stares. The tacit suggestion to these kids was that their futures had already been decided for them. The teachers, like me, were not made of much, and just wanted to bet on the white steed of Caucasia.

Later on that first day, after we were all summoned to an assembly, filing en masse down the stairwell to the auditorium, I felt eyes on my back, though I dared not turn around. Furtively looking about, I met the eyes of a thick-set, mahogany lad, and I knew beyond peradventure that we were, both of us, mongrels; both of us

---

*United States senator Paul Sarbanes had his daughter Janet enrolled there, and they most certainly were not locals.

RESTLESS NATIVES

as he fixed me with a stare and asked, *You mixed?*

My eyes spinning wildly in their orbits, I scanned the faces of my rambling classmates, who seemed lost in their own society. Had they heard his question? He was the only one who'd phrased it thus. He *knew*. But no one looked our way. Something in this boy's tone, or his stormy gaze, would not allow me to lie to him.

I nodded.

Can you fight?

The whole Beverly Sills business barely an hour old, I chose honesty as the wisest course of action. *No,* I mumbled to my shoes.

He nodded curtly. *Then you've got a friend.*

And that would be pretty much that, for the next thirty years.

———◆———

Stefan Templeton and I were opposite sides of the same coin, though he was cast in finer metal. His father was black; his mother was white. Just like me. His father was raising him alone. Just like me and my dad. Stefan's mother, Ebba, was a Norwegian ex-hippie who had moved back to Europe after divorcing Stefan's father, Roye, when Stefan was five. This imbued Stefan with the same tincture of maternal abandonment, though he got a reprieve at the close of each school year, when he would spend summers in Paris, Norway, or London with his mother. Though Stefan had deeper pigment and all the stigma that came with it, he also got a yearly ticket out, which dilated his sensibilities. Upon his return to these shores each September, the America with which he was reacquainted greeted his pigment as a flavor, exotica, a thing of beauty. In Baltimore, he walked above us all.

Stefan Templeton came from a line of notable black Baltimoreans—his paternal grandfather, an educator, had an elementary school named after him. Though Stefan and I shared many similarities, it was our elemental differences that made us friends. I was weak; Stefan was strong. He recognized me as a fellow mongrel, one who would have surely been isolated from the pack and destroyed, whereas he, who was built like a tank, had been a black belt in tae kwon do since, like, the age of seven. He furnished me with my first, and most lasting, model of whatever it means to be a man among men.

We were inseparable and, conveniently, my grandmother adored him. She knew something of his family history and was friendly with Stefan's paternal grandmother, Irene, a beneficent, slightly tetched widow who lived in a luxurious high-rise by Baltimore's inner harbor. The first time I met Irene, as Stefan and I stood in her building's shag-carpeted hallway awaiting an acknowledgment of her long-ago-rung doorbell, he matter-of-factly said, *Don't eat her food.* We were on our way to the annual Baltimore City Fair, held each year on an eyesore of empty land called "Rash Field," which featured rides, games of skill and chance, and boundless merrymaking. My job was to occupy Irene while Stefan slipped into her bedroom and liberated some banknotes (in aid of funding the rides, games of skill and chance, etc.) from her purse. I sat in the living room, a transcendentally benign smile plastered across my mug, while Irene nodded intermittently, and wholly without any context, across the coffee table at me. Fair-skinned and handsome, she resembled a mulatto Julia Childs.

You're nothing but skin and bones—stay there, dear, she threatened before doddering off to the kitchen. I wondered what the hell was keeping Stefan. Irene came back with a can of Coke and a jar of pickles. I snapped open the Coke, dropping the pull-tab into the corrosive elixir. Then delicately, with thumb and forefinger, I pulled a kosher dill from the briny jar and cast a sidelong peeper at the doorway. *Hurry up, Jesus Christ, hurry up.* I was halfway finished with the Coke, the pickle but a memory, when I heard the toilet flush and Stefan sauntered into the living room. He winked at me. *Grammaw, we're going to the fair now.*

Okay, darling, do you need a few dollars? Our eyes locked, then flashed. Fuck it. In for a penny, in for a pound.

Just a couple would be great, we'll win you something. She wobbled into the bedroom. Stefan patted his pocket and gave me a thumbs-up. I thought I saw him give a perturbed glance at the can of Coke and the jar of pickles on the table, but by now Irene was back, *Here you go, darling,* and with the press of her hand, a folded fiver alighted into each of our palms, busses on our cheeks.

Thirty minutes later, as rivers of loose, acrid stool sluiced down my knee-panted legs and into my sweatsocks and Keds, Stefan winced, *Man—I told you not to eat any of her food.*

It was a pickle, I said, as the fairgoers within proximate respiration expanded their berth, *how can a pickle go bad?*

We walked all the way—it was a mile if it was an inch—home. By then I had adopted the lumbering gait of a Frankenstein monster, befouled knees locked and swinging forward, so reviled was I by my own putrefaction that I couldn't bear to have my crusted skin come into contact with itself. Had the situation been reversed, I have no doubt I would have fabricated a rushed apology (something about a deathly allergy to fecal matter) and bade him a hasty *bon chance.* But that was before I knew something about friendship. Stefan walked with me the whole way home. Whenever horrified passersby

came abreast, he made sure to ask me (and this he must
have done a hundred times), in a voice calculated to be
overheard: *Man . . . how did you not see that mud puddle?*

———•———

Ours was a great romance. Stefan was my id, all my
rage and terror honed into muscle, discipline, and
courage. Given the same genetic blueprint, he had
crushed his variations into a diamond. In his society, I
became more than the sum of my own fears. I became in-
vincible.

Roye, Stefan's father, was a Vietnam vet and one of
the first black commissioned naval officers. Roye was in
every way the opposite of Ralph, as I was the opposite of
Stefan. My father greeted every day hunched over the
toilet for a hacking, sputumous session, my own tubercu-
lar rooster. Roye's mornings were inaugurated with a
hundred or so bare-knuckled push-ups, a five-mile jog,
and perhaps (time permitting before work) an elaborate
kata or two. He was six feet two, his hazel-eyed mien resembling a light-skinned version of the cinema star Lee
Marvin. While I had rarely seen my father run, catch a
ball, or move at anything brisker than an urgent bop, I
was awed by Roye's spinning kicks, routines with staffs,
nunchakus, and general bad motherfuckerness. His
limbs were long and ropy, the serpentine muscles and
veins clearly visible through his olive skin. My father was
short, slight, and chronically winded. With the cruel

solipsism only a child could indulge, I harbored the grudge that I had been gypped out of a mother and repaid with only half a father.

Roye belonged to the generation *after* my father's—if my father was a product of Malcolm X, Roye was an iteration of Huey P. Newton.* There was a focus and sobriety characteristic of some black Vietnam veterans—a mixture of martial discipline and militant race consciousness that was difficult to miss. They thousand-yard stared you, *through* you, with no need for the basic social graces (otherwise known as bullshit) that castrated other men. I never saw Roye's intensity in my father's generation of veterans, the alleged "rightness" of their war inuring them to Roye's brand of brittle severity. My dad's quiet was in the service and application of cool; he was at all times possessed of the street hustler's breezy manner, able to glibly defuse or simply avoid confrontation. A black man who had fought a white man's war, Roye kept the armor as well as the scars, living among but not with his countrymen.

Every black belt I met growing up was a black Vietnam veteran. Veterans took the sanction to kill other people (a skill given to them free of charge by the U.S. government, in the hopes that said skills might be stringently applied to their fellow people of color) and

---

*Progenitor of maybe the best quote ever: *A forty-five stops all jive.* Don't bother checking Bartlett's for that one.

brought it home, locked away in duffel bags but never wholly forgotten. Roye and other vets found the structure that martial arts lent to life in racist America antidotal; there were still wars requiring discipline, only the venue had changed.

Impressed as I was by Roye, I didn't really wish he was my father. I liked sleeping late and frittering away afternoons and late nights on *Pippi Longstocking* and *Get Smart*. They never ribbed each other, cracked wise, or cried in the Templeton house. Ninja training and looking for Charlie under the stairs would likely have been more traumatic to someone of my Prufrockian inclinations than whatever good might have been borne from the kind of guidance, discipline, and calisthenics practiced there. It would be a facile relegation to suggest that Stefan, or Stefan and Roye, were the operative brawn, my father and I the effete brains. Roye was a professor of philosophy at the University of Maryland and a former Rhodes scholar; while Stefan, at nine, was dog-earing tomes of Vonnegut and Sartre, I confoundedly wrested what I could from Twain and Stevenson.

For his part, my dad dismissed Roye as a quasi-psychotic post-traumatic stress syndrome alpha male (which he was), and Roye (and Stefan) dismissed my dad as a sapless loser, that most impotent of impotents—a *writer*. The Templetons were *doers*, the men *writers* fashion their heroes from, while my dad was merely an observer, unfit even for the bench.

As a result of his physical training, Stefan's interactions with the urban world were lent a thrilling frisson, proving that violence, or the threat of it, is at its most electric when kept just out of view. Later that year, during show-and-tell (I brought a George Harrison record, composed almost entirely of sitar, earning a unanimous round of blank stares and groans), our homeroom teacher, Mrs. Eberhard, outed Stefan:

I understand you do karate, Stefan . . . would you stand up please?

On the edge of our seats—everybody all pop-eyed and *aww-shit, this should be good*—I felt like Alfred the Butler at Bruce Wayne's unmasking as Batman. Stefan stood up, pushing the chair away from him. He clasped his hands behind his back and awaited further instructions.

Stefan, would you mind showing us a little something?

So silent was the class—the squeak of restive Jack Purcells and the susurrus of corduroy trousers the only sounds above the din of anticipatory calm—as Stefan bent his head in thought for a moment, then leveled his gaze at the teacher and replied:

There's no need.

And he sat back down! I had, as a nine-year-old, docilely fixed my sights on the callow goals of acceptance and approval, while he, when confronted with an opportunity to augment his already mythic persona, had coolly demurred. Nothing could have enlarged his status to a greater extent, not if he had donned a ninja suit and in a blur of deadly pirouettes and open-handed strikes dispatched a squadron of knife-wielding thugs, the fleeting display finished off by a series of triple somersaults across the classroom and out the window. He was like a tawny, diminutive James Bond.

Stefan, the averred black militant, spoke three languages (French, Norwegian, English), thus the black kids could count him as one of their own, at least on a phenotypic and political level, while the whites understood that his unlikely farrago of worldliness was beyond their powers of classification. Plus, Stefan could kick everybody's ass, so that took care of anyone who may have been on the fence. I was a made man at school 66. The brothers spared me any hazing, which would have been relatively benign, though de rigueur for most white kids. The white kids accepted me as one of their own, having no solid evidence to the contrary. I was allowed to pass by an inimitable set of circumstances, which you'd be hard-pressed to find outside of an Atwoodian dystopia. So why didn't he "out" me?

Historically, blacks have allowed each other to pass if they could—a paradoxical *let's get one over on Mr. Bobo,* commingled with tacit simpatico. Or Stefan might have been unaware that I was actively passing, having simply assumed that I shared the same blithe, empyrean aplomb about my racial identity that he did. Denial or sympathy, I found the arrangement quite suitable.

By the winter of 1978, at scarcely six months old (if we adopt a Hindustani interpretation of birth as something akin to consciousness), I was reborn as the Hero Trickster. While not particularly humorous, I nonetheless honed my tatterdemalion "sense of humor" using little more than cribbed bits of timing/delivery/setup/payoff from hoary sitcoms or comedy albums, the ludicrous circumstances in which I found, and placed, myself compelling me to deride and burlesque whatever appeared at the end of my nose. Our English teacher, Mrs. Spenser, may as well have been the emcee, keeping the drunks in their seats between strippers and animal acts.

Mr. Templeton, she warbled, *what is the subject of your book proposal?*

Stefan replied, *Breakfast of Champions*—and here he paused, giving me the beat he knew I needed, my hand already up—as she impatiently answered, *Yes, David?*

Yeah—Mrs. Spenser, can I go next? Mine is on Cap'n Crunch.

Bedlam.

Of course, all this would have been less ironic (though no less humorous) had any of us—save Mrs. Spenser and Stefan, of course—any inkling that Stefan's expertly delivered précis was, in fact, not about a crisped wheat cereal endorsed by celebrity athletes.

I suppose Stefan got a kick out of me, as he himself

had a rather melodramatic bent. I believe this was the European influence exerting itself, a sensibility far removed from my borscht belt comedy stylings. Even his serious moments were heralded with a disquieting frankness, so that one's (if one were as callow and insipid as myself) primary response was laughter, out of discomfort more than anything.

During the first year of our friendship, Stefan's mother, Ebba, came for a visit. Sitting primly in my grandmother's living room, her long, braided ("blond" doesn't adequately describe the shading of her Norwegian mane, somewhere between Silver Queen corn and clouded ice) hair organized along each shoulder, she said very little, her eyes, as blue as a Fijian lagoon, alighting between her son and the boy he loved. I felt not a little uncomfortable. I had thought our respective domestic situations so similar that the appearance of Ebba was like that of a doctor who, having deigned to visit two lads in a cancer ward, tells only one of them that he has been cured. Ebba's visit was banal and pleasant, her whole being so radiant and celestial that that small apartment in this small city in this confining country could not possibly have held her in orbit for long, and by the next day she was gone, back to Europe or the firmament. Stefan met me on the way to school the next morning, and after filling up on provisions (Now&Laters, Chick-O-Sticks, Tastykake Butterscotch Krimpets) from Budlow's Delicatessen, we walked in silence. At one corner, while we waited for the light to change, Stefan pointed to his face, where a saline pearl escaped from his eye, and said gravely: *I cry.* Now, he didn't utter this pronouncement like some drooling, imbecilic Lenny from *Of Mice and Men*; no, he was suggesting that he was as capable of pain and loss and longing as the rest of us anemic poltroons. I wanted to laugh then, laugh until scalding tears fled from my eyes, and the air came in choking breaths. Maybe I would die that way, right out on the street, the Now&Later (which after a moment of delectation contours itself to the roof of one's mouth) suddenly inhaled into my windpipe in the midst of all my panting hilarity, my choking mistaken for a continuation of my mirth, and on the off chance that Stefan was

A) Debilitated by grief at my cruelty

or

B) Not in the midst of kicking and chopping
   the living shit out of me,

would he know what to do? What am I saying?—of course he would effortlessly lift me into his arms and set me upon some clover, a flick of his Swiss Army knife and a sure-handed (and discreet) tracheotomy (the kind with but a hairline scar, and later, in college, when a girl's face was snuggled against my neck, she would look up, my sensual votary's unlined countenance now creased with worry, as her slender finger, whitened with the cold [it was likely winter on the quad at NYU, although I was willing to abase my matriculation to Haverford, or at the very least Swarthmore] traced the lineaments of my tra- cheal scar, *Sweetie . . . what happened there?*), a precise and trenchant insertion of his thick thumb and forefin- ger, the bloodied, glutinous, and offending Now&Later tossed into the clover; the wind coming back to me now; I'm on my feet, bent at the waist, hands on my knees, his hand between my shoulder blades, *Jesus . . . you okay?* and a *that was close wasn't it* laugh the only residue, my bloodless dismissal of his love for his mother a mere bagatelle. But that dream, as all dreams of ridiculous men, was merely the conflation of my own guilt and pet- tiness, until even I could see that his pain *was* quite dif- ferent than my own, that however "sad" he was at the "loss" of his mother, the salt that spilled from his eyes was the product of a paltry four months away from her in either direction, the distance from one's hand to one's heart compared to the blackened nights without Jan and the blued days with Karen.

———◆———

I adapted to the rhythms of life among the elderly quickly. If I had been a typically rambunctious, restive child, I may have found the pervasive *quiet* disconcerting. As it was, the Memorial Gardens Apartments meshed perfectly with my proclivities toward observation, as op- posed to participation. I tiptoed everywhere, silently

closed doors with the mincing caress of a volant maître d',
and, after eight o'clock in the evening, turned the television's volume down to levels inaudible to fruit bats. In el-
evators and hallways, clusters of fogies would grumble to
each other, as though I were invisible, . . . *kids doing
here . . . they know this is an old folks' home? . . . well
where's his mother and father?* I kept my eyes on the indi-
cator button, or on the laces of my sneakers, and said
nothing. Stefan, naturally, felt somewhat hemmed in
during his visits. Playing inside was out of the question.
The place was so confining and funereal, he would have
been like a bear riding a tricycle through a gingerbread
house. There was, however, the garden.

The great hedged-in lawn in the back was draped all
around in cropped bluegrass and moored at one corner by
a weeping willow with a slung bough. It was the perfect
place for two lads to run and jump and play, except for
the fact that there was to be no running or jumping or
playing. The most fervent bits of physical animation of
which the residents were capable—a great dinning and
clashing of canes, walkers, and palsied Rockports—took
place during the late afternoon constitutionals, when the
garden path would fill with the afflicted as if en route to
Lourdes.

Sick of the geriatrics and geraniums, Stefan insisted
that we give equal time to his house. A quick glance at
the map will refresh the memory as to the "safety zone" I
described in relation to Bolton Hill. That glance should

also reveal that 1502 McCulloh Street—Stefan's house—
was decidedly *not* within those parameters, two blocks
beyond Eutaw Place.

The stark differences in the two blocks that separated the sylvan enclave of my grandmother's meadow
from the glass-strewn courtyards of the projects en route
to Stefan's were edifying and unnerving. Sets of hawkish
eyes traced our every step, yet Stefan was oblivious—
these were his "brothers," and in a way I suppose they
were mine, but these were the brothers from *Cooley High*,
and I was more accustomed to the brothers from *Sesame
Street*.

Urban body language, the precursor to crime and the
predicate to action, cannot be taught, but only learned
through experience. Two boys lounging on opposite sides
of the same corner, seemingly discrete, reveal themselves
to be cohorts, pincers attuned to the flow of foot traffic,
closing in concert at the sight of the child/senior/weak-
ling, a pair of old sneakers draped from a lamppost the
advertisement for drug markets—when everything is a
symbol, your survival depends on literacy. That
crucible—the walk from Bolton Hill to Stefan's house—
gave me a preternatural ability to descry myriad shapes
of urban danger. It took all of three and a half minutes to
walk to Stefan's house from my grandmother's—give or
take a hundred years.

1502 McCulloh Street was a huge three-story row
house, with a full basement and a dour patch of square

cement for a "backyard." The Templeton home was always dimly lit, light being somewhat reciprocal in nature, its receipt signaling effective consort with the outside world, and there the outside world was not welcome. In the eight years I visited Stefan's home, I never saw another guest. But I have gotten ahead of myself. Before I would make these keen observations as to the architectural arrangement, luminosity, or lack thereof, and paucity of visitors to the house, I would first have to gain admittance, which was arduous, and not without its perils.

After my virginal, eye-opening journey to the hinterlands of Stefan's neighborhood, he turned the key in his lock, looked me in the eye, and gravely said, *I'm gonna need you to wait here.* He opened the outer door, shut it, and from my perch on the outside stairs I could hear him say, *Dad, I'm coming in, and David's with me.* Then I heard the opening of an inner door, just beyond the vestibule, followed by the frantic grating of claws against hardwood, guttural rumblings and a great gnashing of teeth, joined by urgent, human exertions. Then, silence, before the front door opened a crack, and Stefan advised, *Move slowly, do what we say.* He opened it a few inches wider, just enough so I could slip in, the front door quickly shutting behind me. The inner door to the sanctum sanctorum lay ahead, Roye filling its open frame, his hand wrapped fast around a thick hide collar filled with a snarling, ravening German shepherd named Quasi. I was instructed to move *very* slowly, to avoid Quasi's eyes, and to let my hand dangle, digits curled inward to prevent their removal, in order that she might find me more redolent of friend than foe (or intermezzo). I made it past with only the slightest hiccup, evinced by Roye's stern admonition: *Quaasii*, and the tightening of his fist around her collar. After a few years, I became such a familiar presence that we had the whole "entry procedure" whittled down to a breezy five minutes, though I was never able to, say, venture to the bathroom by myself, saunter unattended into the kitchen for a Fig Newton sandwich cookie, or make any sudden moves in the common areas until Quasi did, eventually, obligingly, die.

Stefan had the coolest—one could scarcely call them toys—shit, as singular, dangerous, and exotic as Stefan himself. His GI Joe dolls were outfitted with European gear—esoteric accoutrements like Uzis instead of the plebeian M16s issued to Yankee Joe, French-style berets, and right-drive transport vehicles. Then there was the passel of foreign toys, games, and candies, their mysterious shapes and alien labels flashing the sounds of hooves on cobblestone and the revelry of gay cafés into my ears, images of little boys bounding after *les ballons rouges* before my eyes. Absent and distant mothers, sapless and psychotic fathers, the ghetto and foraged identities melted away in the megacosmic vacuum of his room.

There were also knives. Lots and lots of knives. Apparently, European lads carried switchblades the way we

Americans carried gum. There were stilettos with pearl/ walnut/plastic grips; daggers that ejaculated their steel from below, the blade arriving in a priapic vertical flash; switchblades that issued their edges in a lateral arc, from the side—these were the coolest, as they gave the blade a slightly slower, more sinister arrival, the enterprise accomplished by an adroit flick of the wrist.

The day after Stefan had given me my choice of switchblade, I surreptitiously removed the weapon from my pocket while in line at the cafeteria. No one was watching, so I thought I might reveal my open palm to Stefan, an inside joke, *we're so fucking cool and they're not*; I had, unfortunately, chosen the side-emanating blade (as it had a bit more of a *Rebel Without a Cause/Blackboard Jungle* leather-jacketed hooligan's feel about it), which meant that as I accidentally depressed the release button while pulling it from my pocket, the centrifugal force catapulted the knife from my hand in a clacking, whirling traverse across the cafeteria floor. Stefan dropped his tray and dove (and I mean full on, face-first, as though heading for home plate) across the linoleum, his ten-year-old frame obscuring the knife until he regained his footing (half a second after he hit the ground, Nadia Comaneci could not have recovered as quickly), and though the proceedings elicited some quizzical stares from students and cafeteria staff alike, no one spied the blade. Although his theatricality might have been a bit over the top, Stefan's concern was not unjustified—possession of such a knife would have been grounds for expulsion, as well as juvenile charges. At a clandestine meeting in the boys' room after lunch, I was demoted to front-opening switchblade status.

By the end of my fourth-grade year, my father moved us to an apartment at 1502 Mt. Royal Avenue, less than twenty-five yards from the door of Mt. Royal Middle School, school number 66. This was a fortuitous move (not for any academic reasons—I was still more often late than on time), and I became a Bolton Hill boulevardier, lingering after school for every playground melodrama, until such diversions fizzled. While my grandmother's apartment was also in Bolton Hill it was *just* four blocks eastward and abutting the border; besides, very few kids lived at that end of the neighborhood. Relocated to the middle of the neighborhood, I was no longer a "commuter," a snappy white boy yukking it up, or a vouchsafed second banana—I was a guy from the neighborhood.

As spring loomed in my tenth year, things were looking up. I was a latchkey kid, which was fine by me (although I did spend many evenings at my grandmother's, on "deadline" nights for the *Afro*, which waylaid my father until two, three, five in the morning), and the weather was getting warmer, finally loosing us from the crippling nival shroud of the "Blizzard of '78." To most of these kids and their parents, many of whom were English or Irish (Protestant, natch), happily married, and residing in their magnificent three-story brownstones, I was an oddity. I too lived in a magnificent brownstone, but mine had been chopped into a six-family dwelling, or quasi-dorm, as had most of the housing on Mt. Royal Avenue, converted to accommodate students of nearby Maryland Institute, College of Art. I had never lived in a house, and found the concept of tiered floors, separate bedrooms, and whole families a bit overwhelming. For this, my friends seemed to regard me with an admixture of envy and pity: envy for my ability to socialize at any time and any hour, and pity for that dreadful moment, six o'clock, when the dinner bell rang.

At the appointed hour, as though each and every **PTA** mom and dad had entered into an unalterable covenant, back doors would be flung open and the canorous chants of *A aaa-lis-onnn, Claa-ire, A d-am* would sound across the park. Bounced balls were left in midair, skateboards parked at angles in the grass, and dramas left in Act 2, while my lone frame in the deserted park conveyed a mute, befuddled, *Hey . . . where'd everybody go?* Dinner was served and it wasn't even dark yet. Dinnertime at my apartment or my grandmother's was the arbitrary moment one decided to open the can of Chef Boyardee, or slide the Swanson's frozen dinner into the oven. It was eaten in front of the TV, on a tray, or on the coffee table, and might occur at any hour between eight and twelve in the evening on school nights (during the weekend, anything went). I disdained those kids and their families their togetherness; it was easier to mock them than to linger in the dusk, watching from the bush as the humans consumed their meals by hearths.

As summer neared, Stefan departed for Europe. Free from his overpowering presence for the first time in months, I was able to, if only for a bit, expand my own personality, which meant sinking further and further into whitehood. The nearness of my home and school presented me with something of a problem: eventually my coevals would see me with my father and my blackness would be discovered. It happened sooner, rather than later, a few weeks into the summer. As I was skateboarding with some friends in the park, my pop walked by, sipping coffee from a Styrofoam cup and smoking a cigarette. Peripherally, I saw him, but kept on, pulling a couple of three-sixties, and a trick or two, followed by a couple of *ooohs* and huzzahs. While I was proud that he had seen me, and had seen me commended by my friends, I was not proud enough to acknowledge the lone black man by the fence clapping gently, cup clenched in his teeth; and when freckle-faced Jimmy Gardiner nudged my arm and asked *Who's that?* I shrugged, *Beats me . . . watch this*, and skated away hard.

Later that summer, I saw an apparition. Scampering through the woodchip pile in the park behind Mt. Royal,

I thought I saw a sandy, familiar Afro pass by some trees. I stopped, panting, and broke away from my friends, my feet leading me on a fixed course to where I thought I had seen my brother Elijah. I got to the trees—nothing. I circled the block—nothing but my friends and the odd punker on his/her way to the university. Had I been more (or even a little) perceptive, I might have chalked it up to guilt. In the space of a year, I had gone from color-blind to blind. Elijah was the last person, aside from my father and my grandma, who had cared for me unconditionally. Assured as I was of Stefan's love, it had after all come with the query: *Are you mixed?* Elijah's had had no such condition. Perhaps it was just the eyelash-wilting heat of the afternoon that had induced the mirage. Tang in the kitchen upstairs would be just the tonic. I opened the apartment door, and naturally did not find Elijah waiting to surprise me behind a corner. There was just my dad, in the living room, on the couch. Next to him, a blue Samsonite and a pyramid of suitcases. Next to those, at the end of a Kool Filter King, was

Karen.

Hey, kiddo, long time no see.

CHAPTER VII

NOT WAVING BUT DROWNING

I am afraid of mice. And rats. And, marginally, bugs, reptiles, or any animal that darts, scurries, or crawls. I would rather confront a federation of Crips in a dark alley or a diseased lion on the veldt than a rodent by the cupboard or a silverfish by the basin. Vermin cannot be controlled and, like violence, they are beyond reason. The apartment at Mt. Royal Avenue had mice. Lots of them. Though we no longer lived in the cramped, muted conditions of my grandmother's, our new bachelor pad was a mixed blessing. I had never seen a mouse before age ten, although once acclimated to the reality of their presence, they were, in fact, *all* I could see.

From my vantage point on the living room floor, a small color television at my feet, my head propped against a pillow, the deathless, garish world of late-seventies network television framed between the valley of my loins, I lay in my own waking torpor, until one day my peripheral vision—nature's tocsin that warns us against the world we cannot face nor discern head on—caught a glimpse of something grey and fast and silent. I stared at the spot where I thought I had seen a flash of *something*, and after I had exhausted a slew of prosaic explanations (dustballs, sunspots, hair that was too long and in need of a trim), I allowed myself to admit the possibility of an animal presence, though I limited those possibilities to the fuzzy and/or cute. *A koala bear? No— a mongoose! A mongoose? Just like in "Rikki Tikki Tavi"— not my first choice for an infestation, but they do have fluffy tails, and they are the mortal enemy of the rat and the snake, and . . . where did I get rat from? No, there are no rats, we're on the second floor, and rats can't climb (can they??), and let's get back to ferrets, and Kipling—Rikki really showed that Nagaina . . .* and this would go on, as I stared fixedly at the spot where I thought I had seen something; seconds, or several minutes may have elapsed, but as all fears that are grounded in the primal—the husband who comes home early one night out of a thousand to the dank musk of coition, his wife's flushed face and the elliptical, viscous stain on the tangle of bedclothes, or the phone call that arrives at four A.M. bearing the caller identification of an elderly parent—mine was based on an ungovernable reality, as the spot contained no scrap of paper, nor ferret, but a vile mouse that darted, unequivocally, halfway into the living room, and then back to the crannies beneath the baseboard heater.

I started violently and scrambled onto the couch, where I danced nervously until I mustered enough courage to dash down the hall, gather my shoes and coat, and race the blocks to my grandmother's. All the way there, every rustling leaf or indistinct shape along gutters stuttered my steps and chilled me.

The following day at school, my friend's maledictions over my squeamishness convinced me to be a man and stay that night at the apartment at Mt. Royal. It was a "deadline" night, which meant that my father would not be home until probably close to dawn. I played outside as long as I could, then let myself into the apartment, warily heated a can of something on the stove, and ate my dinner as watchfully as an inmate snitch in a prison mess hall. Then I watched six or seven hours of television (this time the set was placed on the dresser in my bedroom), until the pictures stopped, the National Anthem blared (there was a time, before cable or round-the-clock programming, when television channels simply went off the air, usually at an hour between midnight and two A.M.), and a snowy static settled upon the screen. I lay abed, an unspoiled copy of *Pippi in the South Seas* upon my chest, and began to read. I had taken the precaution of shutting the door, and stopping the half-inch gap at the bottom with a rolled-up towel, to ensure that I was safe from the feral mice in the living room. Actually, I was hermetically sealed *inside* the room with the mouse that decided to venture forth from beside my dresser. I threw *Pippi*, comic books, Jack Purcells—anything accessible at the mouse's coordinates, but he kept right on making reconnaissance runs. To escape, I would have to walk directly past the dresser in order to get to the door, then stoop to free the door from the impeding towel—delaying actions that would have placed me in lingering proximity to the beast. I sat nonplussed for a beat, before deciding resolutely on a course of action. I started screaming.

I let out a few tentative *heelllps*, before opening up the diaphragm and piercing the night with a *HEEEEEEEEEEELLLLLLLP!* After eight or twenty of these, I saw lights flicker outside my window and heard footsteps clanging against the metal stairs of the fire escape landing. It was the hippie couple from the first-floor apartment below us, kneeling outside my bedroom window. They sleepily, gently, wheedled me into letting them in. First I would have to tell them what was the matter. Well aware that a ten-year-old boy's aversion to house mice might be seen as a frivolous abuse of the early morning calm, I yelled, *Ummm, there's a giant rat in my room!* through the glass at them. By this time, a gaggle of neighbors had gathered on the landing with them to grumble together in a choleric, pajamaed mass in the spring air. The window grate had a padlock on it so I could not open it, nor could I stop calling, though at a more attenuated frequency, for help. It was then that the fire department came. Hats pushed back on their heads, galoshes unfastened, they pushed their way through the crowd and knelt at my window. I heard more officious voices by the front door. *He says there's a rat*, the hippie woman said charitably. The fireman outside the window looked as though he was about to bury his dangling mattock into the area just above my hairline. The voices at the front door knocked insistently. *Son, let us in*, they implored. Then I heard a fireman ask, *What's his name?* and I heard a young woman's voice answer, *David*. I recognized the voice as that of my upstairs neighbor Julie, an Art Institute coed with apple cheeks and honeydew breasts, my first impotent, ludicrous "crush." This was not going to help my already slim chances. *Son,* I heard the fireman by the front door say, *I'm sure you don't want us to break your door down. Your daddy wouldn't like that.*

Oh, go ahead—he won't mind! I yelled back unequivocally, hoping that with my waiver we could get my rescue belatedly under way. Of course, they did no such thing, and after an hour or two of gentle persuasion, I leapt from the bed and flung the door open, admitting the (by now murderous) Baltimore City Fire Department, a handful of groggy neighbors, as well as the winsome Julie.

This was how deeply the terror of the unknown had affected me in the presence of a mouse weighing less than four ounces and occupying a space on this planet no greater than three inches, which is rather a circuitous manner of my asking you to imagine, after all that, how I must have felt upon seeing Karen, the other great named terror of my life, sitting in my living room on that summer afternoon.

Obviously, I *had* seen Elijah that day. He, Karen, and Khari had made the same move from Adelphi to Baltimore that my dad and I did, and now they would be living with us. Karen moved into my father's bedroom, Khari moved into mine, and Elijah slept on the couch in the living room. In the year since we had arrived in Baltimore I went from brother to only child, victim to impervious sidekick, black and white to white. No way was I going back. In the meantime, Karen seemed oddly defeated, the slump in her shoulders and the laxity of her bearing conveying an *okay, you win*. Sagging under the burden of single motherhood, she resumed a (much calmer) version of her original relationship with my father. On the rare occasions that their bedroom door opened I would see the ceiling of stale cigarette smoke that hung like nimbus clouds, or boxes of Entenmann's Raspberry Danish Twist, which, between puffing, copulating, and caffeinating, they seemed to subsist on.

I felt no anger toward my father at Karen's return. This new, big, bad city rendered her merely an agrestic, toothless ex-harridan in search of child support and some cock. For once, I was the abandoner, and the taste was not only sweet but lingering. I knew that she would not touch me again. I had my grandmother, blocks—not miles—away; I had Stefan and karate and knives. A week after she arrived, I was bouncing on the bed, hopped up on sugar (Nutter Butter creme sandwiches), when the Karen I knew and had once feared showed herself. *You have to stop that!* she warned, her hands curling. Now—a few months earlier, my math teacher, Mrs. Tolliver (black), had responded to young (white) Gene Hall's assertion that *you have to take another look at my quiz 'cause I think I got one right and you marked it wrong*, with a slight roll of the neck and a lyrical *Have to?* before offering a chestnut, as good as any I'd ever heard, that I stored away for some winter when I found myself on the wrong end of the dozens. Winter came early. I gave the mattress another bounce or two for good measure, my green eyes locked on to her baby blues, and said *Karen, all I have to do is stay black and die.**

———◆———

There was little chance that my recently reunited family (Elijah and Khari) would compromise my identity, because most of my Bolton Hill friends, as summer blazed, were off at band/French/soccer camp, or else summering in Nantucket or Europe, or at the local country club (no, I'm not kidding). Besides, in order to facilitate their rutting season, Karen and Ralph (though I

---

*Okay, I know that I was, by this time, passing. But Karen and I had a history predicated on ugliness, which, at its core, is unerringly honest. I owed her, after our brutally honest history, payment in kind. That would be the last time I referred to myself as black for many years—but what a way to go.

suspect rather more the former) shuffled the three of us off to YMCA summer camp for the last few weeks of the season.

Elijah and I were close enough in age that we were in the same troupe, while Khari went to wherever five-year-old campers go. The YMCA was an "urban" camp, which meant that we walked there (I have mentioned Baltimore's size, but the *smallness* of it all, both in temperament and geography, bears repeating) every weekday morning at nine, and returned home every day at five, as if recreation was our day job. As though we had not skipped a beat Elijah and I were very close; he seemed to sense that even though he and Khari had had a loving mother in Karen, I didn't, so he viewed my departure as regrettably necessary. At camp, Elijah took some delight at having two very light-skinned brothers, as though his role as our dark protector made him a complicated and irreducible grandee. He was genuinely proud to be the darkest part of our spectrum. To me, in my white world, the hint or suspicion of blackness was death. To Elijah, who loved his mother with the rabid loyalty his race demanded, his miscegenation was a source of pride. His mother's whiteness, and the lightness of his brothers, must have made him feel as if he were a ne plus ultra brother for having been touched by the master race, while I took only a sense of abasement from the blood of slaves that ran weakly through my body.

I seem to remember aqueous days spent in the Y's

basement pool, all of us withered raisins (I a sultana) bobbing in a sea of green. Stewart, a fellow camper, was a very pale black boy, bordering on albino, with a nearly blond Afro and freckles; rather than looking white, he merely looked drained of almost all pigment. Stewart attached himself to another camper, a ruddy boy, a doppelgänger for the red-haired friend of Arnold Drummond from the television series *Diff'rent Strokes*. Stewart and let's call him (for shits and giggles) Peter did everything together. I knew what Stewart was about before Stewart knew what Stewart was about, which is to say that just as I saw the carapace of cheer Stewart presented to his artless pal, I also saw the cracks in the edges, the rancor lying in wait. After Stewart lent Peter his diving mask (yes, it was a swimming pool, but snorkeling off the Maldives was not in our budgets) and Peter had had the temerity to accidentally rend the strap from its holder, Stewart snatched the mask back and hissed, his back to the lad, *I don't need some white boy messing up my shit.*

I felt half-ashamed that I had been privy to their interaction, but I had no choice: a watcher, the wreckage of life was something I was helpless to pass by. I was disquieted by Stewart's outburst, but not surprised. America had demonized black skin until black culture itself had become possessed, casting out its devils in a reflexive reclamation of Black as Beautiful, Black as Power. With his deathless Afro and pallid melanin, Stewart had had it even rougher than I. He was ridiculed *and* accepted by his black brothers, while at the same time, whites viewed him as no more, no less, than black. At least I could hide in plain sight. By dint of rage, Stewart needed to make himself blacker, which gave him control over the very thing about himself that he hated. His rudimentary approach was, sadly, successful, for moments later Peter sniffled to himself, and to the water below his chin, . . . *I ever do to that coon?*

Racism is not blindness; it is sight that refuses to be clouded by the heart and mind.

———•———

Bloom now off the rose of her relationship with my father, September found Karen and Elijah in an apartment east of the city, while Khari stayed with my father and me. Karen became solely a weekend presence, my dealings with her limited to the depositing and recollecting of Khari upon and from her doorstep at the beginning and end of each weekend. Khari was a new addition to Mt. Royal 66, the five years separating our grades dog years in terms of compatibility. Besides, Stefan had returned, and I was becoming a real fifth-grade presence, a cynosure among the tightly knit clique of white kids. Neither a fashionable kid nor a geek, I was an odd bird somewhere in between. While there weren't enough white (rich—same thing) kids at Mt. Royal to establish an in-crowd, there were enough to infect the white ranks with "preppy" fashion, which reached ludicrous heights during the late seventies and early eighties.

Even before that odious trend caught fire, Baltimore's white upper class (gentiles, at least) had preppy inclinations. Bolton Hill had plenty of foot soldiers of the preppy movement, who favored the preppy (we called them "preps") diversions like swimming, tennis, soccer, and that witless endeavor practiced by a graceless race incapable of the fade-away: lacrosse. White people love(d) lacrosse for the same reason black people hated it: it involves a host of medieval equipment, cold mornings, brittle soil, and the willingness to look inelegant in front of others. The preps wore Izod shirts, Levi's jeans (although some of the more "artistic" kids—sons and daughters of well-to-do ex-hippies—subverted the trend by wearing formless Oshkosh B'Gosh overalls), and above all Nike shoes with the light-blue stripe against white canvas. I stayed out of this fray as long as I could, avoiding all of the trappings save the shoes.

During lunch one day, the Williams sisters, two identical twins (they were also adopted, adding a layer of schmaltzy *scandale* to their existence) and the only Jews I was aware of at 66, bounded over to my table with a Nike tennis shoe box, which they presented with a flourish to my friend Craig Harbourt.

Craig was a long-haired transplant from Rochester, New York, whose English mother was an associate professor at the Maryland Institute of Art. Craig was funny, in a wry Canadian sort of way, expert at mimicry and a well-timed pratfall. He was self-deprecating about his and his mother's starving artist status, and his own threadbare clothes. The first time I went to Craig's basement apartment (we were playing hooky) I raided his fridge, picking under the foil at a desiccated piece of chicken breast. From behind me, he joked, *C'mon, that's our dinner tonight*, and I laughed. I know now that he was not joking, but I knew only black and white then, white equaling have, so I reasoned that Craig and his mother must have had food and the means to get it. Solitary fowl in the icebox or not—white people did not go hungry in my America.

Even if one was not a preppy, name-brand sneakers—Nikes especially—were fast becoming the one arbiter of class that could not be ignored. When asked about the brand name of his supermarket-bought shoes, Craig would gamely deflect the question by running madly back and forth around the inquisitor, *These are Action Shoes!* Vulnerable to attack as I was from the exertions of my passing, I knew my puddinglike psyche could not withstand a direct attack on my family's solvency, so I resolved to get myself a name-brand pair of sneakers if it killed me. During our yearly trip to the shoe store (I received a new pair, once a year, at the beginning of the school year), my father asked the salesman where the sneakers were. The salesman (commend his soul to

Christ!) plopped a pair of Nikes on the counter. I had never even touched a pair, and here they were. My father pulled his gnarled wallet from his back pocket and prepared to pay. I could barely control my bladder I was so nervous, but I was my father's son, and cool I would be. *That'll be twenty-four fifty*, the salesman said, and my father's wallet snapped shut with the precipitous ire of an unpaid whore. *Hell no*, he said, pointing toward a metal bin by the front door containing a jumble of sneakers made from what looked like used chewing gum and waxed canvas. He chose a pair—the abominations were tied together at the eyelets by their own laces—checked the price ($9.95), and we were on our way. The next day, after my father had gone to work, I wheedled my grandmother into a cab and out into the suburbs to a fancy shoe store, describing to her, in painstakingly specious detail, how my gym teacher had informed me that I might be a fine sprinter if I took the right precautions with my feet. I brandished a pair of Adidas—*no one* had these at school (I recognized the brand from Stefan's closet of European wonders, and knew them to be of quality)—under my grandmother's nose and displayed for her the benefits of the rubber arch, the suede body, and the plenitude of suction cups along the sole. Thirty-two dollars later—*You can't put a price tag on your feet, Gramma—the first medal's for you!*—and we were gone.

While *I* escaped foot-related peer pressure, the cruelty of preadolescence would not humor Craig for much longer. The preppies and the Williams sisters—Izod collars turned up against their Farrah flips, whale-stained turtlenecks—had it out for Craig, the only obviously poor white kid at 66.* Craig opened the shoe box and pulled out a worn pair of Nike tennis shoes. But the Williams sisters weren't done yet: they had lined the shoe box with hundreds of handmade (like they'd ever seen one) food stamps. Ann Williams (or maybe Laura?) grabbed a handful, raining them down on Craig like confetti.

Though he was equable, making some joke or another about *I wonder if the cafeteria accepts these?* I was wounded for him, and for the Williams sisters too, because I knew that I would exact a punishment on them that would make the hours they had spent drawing, cutting to size—dreaming up this whole lurid business— seem like a rest stop at Dante's Judecca. I turned one of the "food stamps" over in my hand and, as the laughter died down, said to the sisters, *Oh, jeez, how could I forget? You were supposed to go to the principal's office . . . something about how your real mother only gave you up 'cause she thought you were stillborn, and she feels real bad, and stopped by to say she wants you back, but then she found out you were Jews and said never mind*, to which one or both almost immediately started weeping. I took my vengeance, and the backslaps, and the raucous laughter of

---

*Save one student named Robert, whose acquaintance we will make shortly.

my peers, but I did not take any credit. All I had really
done was project the fury of my own abandonment into
the air, like an oath against God. I was glad someone
found it funny.

There were two cats living with us at Mt. Royal, ac-
quisitions from a local spinster who had a boxful of kittens. Elijah and I each picked one, he a golden tom, me a
calico tabby, and with that the mouse problem was immediately solved. I thought then that I could happily
live forever between the Mt. Royal apartment and my
grandmother's. By my sixth-grade year, Elijah was in junior high somewhere, and Khari was safely immured in
the bowels of Mt. Royal 66, as I glided toward upper-
classman status (our school continued to the eighth
grade). Stefan was my primary mate, but the Bolton Hill
kids were my everyday running buddies. The edges of the
city had yet to creep into our world, although the increasingly frequent raids by the black kids from just outside Bolton Hill's borders were harbingers that whatever
world we occupied was not the real one.

Though Stefan and I no longer had to play at my
grandmother's, the fallow brownstones and cobbled lanes
of Bolton Hill were no better fit for him. So I continued,
on those occasions I couldn't get out of it, to make the
trek to his house. If I had to go alone (I almost never

agreed to that Faustian bargain) I usually waited until nightfall, figuring that I could use the shadows as cover; sometimes this worked, other times it didn't. One afternoon, my fear surpassing my pride, I begged Stefan to walk me home from his house, a request that left him bemused and not a little ashamed of me. Proud in an era quite given over to vainglory, Stefan stood ramrod straight (never mind adults—how many eleven-year-olds can resist the all but requisite slouch that accompanies preadolescence?) and viewed the street, much like the dojo, as a place where one is composed, forthright, and gives no quarter. Even as pipsqueaks, as I would amble and he would stride down a city street, when we crossed paths with other boys, or even men, Stefan would walk *through* them—no matter how many of them there were. This movement requires some forensic inspection. Usually, when two hominids come abreast of each other, one must step aside, or at least twist the body in order to accommodate the other's passing. Not Stefan. Accommodation, *making way*—that was the other guy's job. It makes sense. On the street, the real estate under your feet is the only indication that you, in fact, exist. Stefan, in a simple assertion of person and place, was an existentialist.

The Bruce Manor Housing Projects (see map legend) stood between Bolton Hill and Stefan's house. On the night Stefan agreed to walk me home, he suggested we take the path right through the housing projects, the one route—both quicker and more direct—that I *never* took. Halfway across the squat cement complex, Stefan suddenly veered toward an entrance to a cluster of apartments. Opening the door, he urged me to *come on.* I bit my lip, stuck. He was testing me, right here in the middle of enemy territory. If I declined to follow Stefan into that building, I'd have to make it out of the projects by myself. If I did follow him, well . . . I'd be inside the projects.

I could sense him measuring my heart the whole way up the stairs.

I just gotta say hi to a friend, he said.

No problem, I blustered.

As we passed the next landing, I heard a woman's voice, throaty and insistent: *Hit that nut, hit that nut, hit that nut.* Then I saw her on her knees, a man, bloated and sleepy and with his pants around his ankles, standing above her while she worked feverishly with lips and fingertips. The pocked, ochre woman, her straightened hair in ragged perpendicular shelves against her head, saw Stefan, then winked. With his lifeless, dead eel of a cock in her hands, the man grunted, *'Sup, youngblood?* to Stefan, who grunted, *'Sup?* right back.

I kept my eyes on each step coming up to greet me, impelled by the vacuum of Stefan's slipstream. Turns out the friend wasn't home.

In the summer of my eleventh year, my father and I were driving back from a late-night meal at the Howard Johnson's when he said, *How'd you like to see your new house?* Though I had seen my father's weekly pay stubs from the *Afro* ($332.69, after taxes) I vouchsafed my *okayyy*.

We pulled up to the 1400 block of Madison Avenue— the Bruce Manor apartments fifty feet to our left, Stefan's house catty-corner across the street—and I stayed in the car, slunk low in the seat, while my father inspected the front of house number 1423. I knew then that whatever else had happened to me in the previous eleven years, this was

not

going

to

be

all right.

CHAPTER VIII

HARVEST HOME

While my father fiddled with the lock inside the vestibule, I waited on the marble steps of our new house. This autumn day, a few weeks since I laid eyes on the place, but still a few months before we moved in, would mark the first time I had seen 1423 Madison Avenue during the daytime. A couple of teenage black boys walked by and started singing *Play that funky music, white boy.* Sneaking a look, I caught one of them lifting his T-shirt to expose the walnut grip of a pistol shoved into his waistband. He smiled and nodded, the duo never breaking their perfect two-part harmony. My father, who was still hunched over the lock, hadn't noticed. If he had he probably would have told me to go make friends with those guys, because *you need to know all kinds of people.*

I think I'll wait in the car, I said, without waiting for an answer. Just as I pulled open the passenger-side door, a reedy, dark-skinned boy of about sixteen ambled by and, almost as an afterthought, in the way he might have snapped his fingers at the recollection of a sink left running, stopped and turned. *You wanna fight?*

I . . . I . . . no . . . I stammered. Was he *joking?*—at

over six feet tall he was a man. I was but four foot eight—
and no more than sixty-five pounds soaking wet, clutching a brick.

My father swung the door open. *Yo, Dave! I got it*,
he called, oblivious. The boy glowered at me through
hooded lids, an impatient *well?* still etched across his
face. I stared at the cracks in the sidewalk until he
shrugged and walked off. I prayed that I would never
see him again, but prayers, like curses, depend on the
cruelties and kindnesses of demons or gods, which do
not exist. Black boys who look white, and the black
boys who hate them, do, and would meet up again before too long.

1423 Madison Avenue was a real fixer-upper: no electricity, no plumbing, no heat. The walls were made of
cracked and pocked plaster, the wood lathe showing
through. In those places where they existed at all, the
floors were minefields of rotted pine. My heart sank,
pumping an admixture of rage and self-pity. How could
my father do this to me? This was not a place someone
(*were those mold spores I smelled?*) of my disposition could
live. I'd already been threatened twice in as many minutes, once on pain of death, marked simply for *existing*, a
condition I was just then at a loss to ameliorate. Hours
earlier, and two blocks over, white meant life—or at least
the kind I, after examining my options, had deemed
worth living—but now it seemed my death sentence.

The house did have size going for it: three full stories

plus a basement, backyard, five bedrooms, two stairwells (one grand staircase and a "servants" staircase that snaked through the rear of the house), two bathrooms, and a potbellied coal furnace in the basement. Twenty-five hundred square feet of faded glory. While my father regaled me with *they just don't make 'em like this anymore* gasconade, I realized that I clearly needed to act fast.

Which bedroom do you want? he asked, his earnestness rocking me. He bought this house not for himself but for me. Wavering, I poked my head through the doorway of a room big enough for my adventures and my books (essentially one and the same), and for a moment the mottled wallpaper and splintery floors seemed redeemable. Then I heard it. Faint. Insistent. The sinister bass line and bell-bottomed ritornello of Wild Cherry's only hit came back and hit me hard, *play that funky music*. So much for my short-lived attempts at conciliation or renovation. Force-fed gazpacho and stinging open fists were altogether different than Saturday Night Specials and coarse bare knuckles. I didn't know much about realty, or the stages of tenancy, but perhaps the "paperwork" hadn't yet been signed. *Hold fast*, I told myself—this may not yet be written in stone; maybe we could still back out of it. I would, however, have to soft-sell my reluctance: my father knew all too well that I was an inveterate contrarian.

Be careful over there, Pop—floor looks a little shaky, I

cautioned. Looking out for his best interest. Such a good son. I ostentatiously wiggled banisters, heroically struggled with rusted window sashes, guilelessly tapped crumbling patches of plaster—jumping back with mock alacrity as a tectonic slab crashed at my feet—the whole "kicking the tires" charade attended by a prudent half-frown, a silent adviso that *we needed to be practical about this, old man—can't go throwing our investments around willy-nilly,* and *oh well, it had been a lovely idea, perhaps a little pied-à-terre a bit farther to the east—I'll wait while you drop off the keys.*

Unmoved, he led me to the basement, and in that dank cave I confronted what I must have known was there, from the moment we had broached the threshold: the withered corpse of a giant Norway rat.

———◆———

My father had managed, with his mother as co-signatory, to secure a mortgage on a three-story house with marble stairs for the sum of $10,000. During the early eighties, Baltimore had begun the sale of what the city administration had referred to as "dollar houses": houses in run-down neighborhoods, the ludicrous pricing a last-ditch effort to stave off complete urban blight. My father had grown up mere blocks from 1423 Madison Avenue, and so wistfully, if also willfully, saw in this purchase the reclamation of his youth, or, more grandly, that of a bygone era when this block was a hub of black middle-classdom.

But times done changed. The neighborhood was still black, but was now also poor, its forsaken, if elegant, apartment buildings supplanted by cheerless housing projects, familiar shopkeepers replaced by Korean proprietors of liquor stores, where transactions were handled through bulletproof glass.

Gone was the noble era of the *Baltimore Afro-American* newspaper, and the grand minister's house my father had lived in as an infant, gone was the Bellview Manchester, where Mae and Ivy had resided among professionals and families, all replaced by the carrion of abandoned buildings, the plywood on their windows like pennies over the eyes of the dead.

I had never, and haven't since, beheld such a dramatic and precipitous disparity in the fortunes of a single city block. Were I (like my father) a conspiracy theorist, I could easily reach the conclusion that there must be some *design* to the arrangement. The houses across Eutaw Street were just as grand, and every bit as soundly constructed, as any manse in Bolton Hill. The only difference was that across Eutaw, the houses were filled with black people. I had heard of the wrong side of the tracks, but Jesus—the wrong side of the street?

I had lived in Bolton Hill. Now I lived in the ghetto. If inches were miles or years, the space between those two sentences is nearly to scale.

The *Baltimore Afro-American* was founded in 1892 by John Murphy, a former slave, and would attain a level of prominence under the stewardship of John's son, Carl (remember Violet—my grandmother's roommate—Carl's personal secretary?). By the time my father commenced his role as managing editor in 1977, ownership had been passed down yet again to John Murphy III. As a child, I had begun a habit of shunning newspapers the way Holden Caulfield avoided the movies; nonetheless I bestowed a dim veneration upon my father's métier, the way one detachedly esteems a haberdasher, or a first timpanist.

I was peripherally familiar with Baltimore's paper of record, the *Baltimore Sun* (where my grandmother had worked for a moment in the twenties), and *that* daily looked like what I had supposed a paper ought to: crisp photographs above the fold, neatly trimmed edges, august headlines staring out from behind endless, cycloptic vending machines. By contrast, I remember the feel of the *Baltimore Afro-American*'s coarse, translucent newsprint like a shock to the ass accustomed to Charmin now receiving Scott tissues, the grainy photos below the fold, and most of all the ink, so cheap and runny, which blackened the hands, a black impossible to wash away. I visited the cavernous offices of the paper often, though only when I couldn't get out of it. Even without any idea of what a newspaper's offices were supposed to look like, I decided that the space had an antediluvian quality, like a secondhand shop for printers, or a museum.

On the first floor was the "head" of the paper: the switchboard and the "money desk," where advertising space could be purchased on a walk-in basis; behind that, the lower intestines—printing presses, a whirring symphony of violent machines and nimble men, all caked with black ink and skin, expelling the bundled copy into the distribution bays at the rear of the building. On the second floor were the hands: the teletype room, and an alcove that bore the sign Morgue, which never failed to induce a shudder in me, even after I discovered its true meaning. Finally, at the end of the third flight up the narrow stairway, the heart of the paper, the city desk. In the forties, during my father's first incarnation at the *Afro*, I'd been told that there had actually been a single desk— a large horseshoe of wood and steel—around the outside of which all the reporters labored, the editors directing their efforts from the inside. By the time I made my acquaintance with the *Afro*, reporters occupied sovereign desks, archipelagos strewn across the third floor, each representing a different section of the paper—sports, society, metro, or metro beat, or something to that effect— and then, rear center stage, my father's desk presiding over them all.

I never noticed the Pirandellian dramas playing out all around me, the microcosm of black politic maneuverings, deal making, and survival. Councilmen, criminals (you would be surprised how often they shared the same skeletons), and everymen circulated through the dusty newsroom, glad-handing, wheedling, or outright beseeching in their pleas for inclusion within, or coventry from, the folds of the paper. One time, my father's *gimme five minutes, Dave*, had predictably seen dusk turn to inky night. While I sighed and pouted in judgment of these people temerarious enough to work toward the education and uplift of their race (a lost cause, I reckoned, if ever there was one), an aged, towering black man, hunched into a permanent apostrophe, shuffled to my father's desk. He stood there for a moment, trying to collect or give voice to his thoughts, as my father waved him into the chair beside his desk. I could not hear what the man was on about; he clutched a beaten shoe box under the arm of his threadbare sports jacket and seemed quietly agitated. My father listened attentively, interjecting empathetic *mm-hmm*s, and *I know that's right*s at regular intervals. My father had a way, though it was less limited to his person than it was confined to the black community, of commiserating with another's woes or outrages with a prompting grunt. That *mm-hmm*, or *mm-ph!* was a truncated version of the *preach, nigger!* or *go, on!* heard from Jesus-soaked, fanning believers on Sunday mornings. After a length, my father said, in his soothing, Verdi baritone, *Yes, sir . . . you know, if you leave that with me, I can take care of all this; don't you worry your mind.* The man handed the box over before being walked to the stairway by my father, his consoling palm along the small of the man's stooped back. As they disappeared from view, I heard the low hum of my father's reassurances, and saw the mollified profile of the old man, who received the words like benedictions. When I was sure they were both out of sight, I wandered over to my father's desk, my finger just under the lid of the shoe box—*Get the hell away from there!*—my father threatened, snatching it from me while instructing his secretary to call the police. When they came to retrieve the gun (which I never did see), my father told them he had found it on the sidewalk in front of the building. He never mentioned the old man. As we left the *Afro* that night, I asked my father if the old man had come there to kill him (which would have been a tantalizing bit of intrigue—I pictured myself at school the next day with Stefan by my side: *Yup, things got pretty rough last night at the paper—the old man disarmed an assassin*) and he replied that the man had *only wanted someone to tell his troubles to.*

Fool that I was, I did not realize that the *Afro*, and the black press in general, did more than merely produce a paper for their readers: it was a place to tell your troubles. The white press had a lock on the money, the last word, and those crisply photographed and neatly trimmed truths, truths they had—in concert with their legion of advertisers—ratified by dint of their publication, nothing more. The white press's truths were not the whole truths, and the *Afro* was proof that occasionally the earth, even in Baltimore, did not revolve around the *Sun*.

It was cues like those, which told the story of money/power/access and race (and reductively, they are the same thing in our little America), that constantly reaffirmed my decision to pass. In my ignorance, I felt that there was something *subpar* about the black iterations of the American experience—the *Afro* would never be the *Sun*, just as Kwanzaa would never be Christmas.*

Owing to his late nights spent at the *Afro*, my father briefly hired a babysitter to watch over Khari and me when we lived at the apartment on Mt. Royal Avenue. Priscilla Genarro was a Maryland Institute student, a pudgy girl with Little Orphan Annie curls who wore denim skirts pulled taut around her hips. Her roommates were two other coeds, shrill painters who smoked and gossiped through the afternoons and into the evenings, their overalls splattered with creations finer than any they committed to canvas. Occasionally, Priscilla took us back to her place. One night, while Khari and I waited for my father to come pick us up (he was, as usual, egregiously late), I heard Roommate A ask, *Why's he always so late picking them up?*

Roommate B answered, *He works at the* Afro-American . . . with that, I shushed Khari and cracked

---

*Let's be real—Kwanzaa is a bullshit lesser holiday, up there with Hanukkah and Earth Day.

the door an inch, just as Roommate A sneered—as though she'd been offered a bloody Tampax on an hors d'oeuvre tray—*What's that?*

Roommate B replied, with nose-wrinkling disdain, *Some black paper.* She spat *black* out as though the word, if left too long on the palate, might defile her tongue, bedimming the new moon of pearly, expensively arranged teeth around it. I hesitated at the door, torn between marching out and demanding of those effete, subsidized cunts, *Yes, and what of it?!* or shutting the door silently, adding their cancer to my own. With the preceding decade I have laid before you, dear reader . . . can you guess which option I chose?

I wanted access. I wanted the benefit of the doubt. I wanted in on the America that smiled back at me from my television and from my teacher's encouraging glances, from shopkeepers and policemen, from apple-cheeked parents and their hale offspring, from dark-skinned secretaries (*such good hair!*) and light-skinned grandmothers (*poor dahkies*). This America smiled back at blacks, but it was more the indulgent smile of a listener who, having already heard the joke, waits patiently for the punch line. I knew that there really was only one thing to be in Baltimore, America, and that was white. Blacks were tacitly marked for extinction, summoned meekly to mountaintops (*I might not get there with you . . .*). I wanted the America that, having been disingenuously promised to all, had unwittingly been granted to me. I wanted the run

of the house, not the field. Life for me was not a war between black and white, or rich and poor, it was a life sentence that could be commuted only by whiteness, real or
imagined.

Too poor to hire a contractor, my dad undertook the
renovation of The House himself. Or should I say, himself
plus me and Elijah, who was delighted. He outfitted us
with crowbars and cotton masks, and in a blink our weekends disappeared. A teenager by now, Elijah found succor in sanctioned destruction. I was less than thrilled.
The crowbar (the smallest one made) weighed about as
much as I did and gave me calluses. I spent weekend after
reluctant weekend on either Plan A: shirking my half of
the duties; or Plan B: reluctantly banging down walls,
pulling apart rotting wood, and scraping hundred-year-
old wallpaper off plaster. I would vomit great globs of
soot and grime, dry-heaving the inhaled bits of the building after tearing it apart left nothing in my gut. We pulled
a quarter ton of lathe, joists, and plaster of paris from
the house, many Mazdas' worth of refuse for the city
dump. We (ineptly) put up Sheetrock, nailed down slabs
of plywood flooring, and welded copper in aid of a potable
water source and yet still barely made a dent. As each
Saturday resembled the last, I began to wonder if malev-
olent elves were undoing the previous week's paltry efforts while we slept. We pissed in the kitchen sink—there

was no kitchen save for a sink, the most elaborate bit of construction we had been able to pull off—and stored our bowel movements for more accommodating venues.

When I couldn't finagle a sleepover at my grandmother's, I slept in the room I had chosen on the third floor, as it was farthest from the rats. From the ceiling, an extension cord with a lightbulb screwed to its end hung like an IV, providing a blood drip of light to keep rats from my bed and the pages of my books. In the moments between turning those pages, reports of gunfire issuing outside my window, I wondered why my father had consigned us to this existence. Was he so benighted as to believe that "gentrification" (we heard that word constantly during those years, but only from him) would seep westward from Bolton Hill? Or did he believe that I would adapt and be adopted by our black neighbors, finally evolving into a robust, magnanimous plebian? Or was he simply trying to juggle his son's providence against his mother's survival?

——————◆——————

While we were living in the apartment on Mt. Royal Avenue, my grandmother received a slight reprieve from her duties as primary caregiver. As she never failed to bemoan, she had survived two heart attacks before Khari and I were born, and we were forever "getting her pressure up." Khari was good-natured and rambunctious, generally amenable to *being a good boy*, while I was crafty and manipulative. Yet my grandmother loved me most of all, even in the midst of my deviltry.

My impudence (her word) was generally confined to the area of the television. She was a six o'clock news fiend. That was a problem. I didn't get home from school until two forty-five or so, and thenceforth sat immobile in front of the tube. My favorites, the more "adult" reruns, began at five, the cartoons immediately prior to the *amuse bouche*. The lineup was *Gilligan's Island*, at five P.M., *Gomer Pyle, USMC* at five-thirty, and at six, the crown roast, *Get Smart*. Then the lovely petit four selection of *The Andy Griffith Show*, which aired at six-thirty, by which time the news had already been on for thirty minutes with another thirty yet to go. You see, at around five-thirty or so, my grandmother's internal clock impelled her to call out from the bedroom, *Is it time for the six o'clock news?** Khari strained against his upright sense of honesty, while I was free from any such compunctions. *Nope,* I would call out, *it's only five-thirty!* when it was, of course, six twenty-five. If Khari squirmed or otherwise made any motions toward disclosure, I either bribed or beat him.

Television was the world in which I felt most at home. There was a homogeneity of peoples and places, all that white skin, straight teeth, and blinding California

---

*Eventually, they came out with a five-thirty edition (!), and my sophistry became as complex as Chinese arithmetic.

sun. The sufferings there were ephemeral and slight, solvable within thirty or sixty minutes. Things were *ordered*. The world was *thus* and *so*. I was a living contradiction of elements that shouldn't have been, with no neat place to arrange them; the sighing, beatific perfection of TV was the place to rest my superego. In its phosphorescent glow, everything was black, or white, and a lot like life.

By eleven o'clock the viewing cycle would be repeated, as the "serious" shows required my attentions. Exasperated at her day's lack of access to the "Eyewitness News" with its witless reportage of oppidan scandals and minatory apocalypses, my grandmother was a wreck by bedtime. But *Barney Miller, M*A*S*H,* and *Good Times* were every bit as important to me as my afternoon serials, and asking me to choose only one was akin to asking me whether I should prefer to pluck out my eyes or puncture my eardrums. At eleven, after I had spent an afternoon and evening in front of the television (I once calculated my daily intake, including summers and weekends, at eleven hours per day), she would renew her entreaties to watch the eleven o'clock news, which I would dismiss—often with a theatrical parting of the venetian blinds and check of the street below, the sky above: *Nope—no bombs, no sirens—so much for the news!* My grandmother would sigh, and enjoin: *That's all right . . . wait till your fathah gets home . . . you'll see,* to which I would reply, *Hmm-mhm,* for I knew that at four A.M., when he did, asking his mother how her day went would be very low on his list of priorities. By ten fifty-nine, when it looked as though the nightly news would truly go as unobserved as the evening edition, she would demand fervidly: *Do you want me to die!?* I didn't doubt her sincerity, but these moments of Grand Guignol were nevertheless wasted on me—I was the son of her son, my response to hot emotion glacial remove.

Mae and I shared a bed, which never struck me as odd (even if it did strike me as just creepy enough that I never mentioned it to anyone), and many nights I would listen to her breathing, shallow and protracted, imagining each one as her last. I often tried to picture my grandmother dead—pupils fixed and depthless, mouth slack, her fluids wicking into the box spring, rigor mortis seizing her tiny hands into claws—in order to prepare for it, make the event a formality, leaving me already through the worst of it. I could never succeed in making her a "short-timer" in my mind because, in an innate, nearly Cartesian sense, I could not imagine or conceive of life without her. The others who lined the halls of Memorial Gardens would and could die, but I was young and would live forever and a lifetime; and in this way Apartment 413 would be spared by the lamb's blood of my will.

My father instructed Khari and me that we would be gone from the apartment on Mt. Royal by the Christmas break and, in fact, we were. The day we moved into The

House, the December air was cold and grey, but my father was not in the least bit worried. We had the miracle fuel—*Coal!*—to keep us warm. The beast in the basement was what folks had used (in the fucking Mesozoic era) to heat their homes. Oil? . . . Electricity? *Pshaw!—you want heat? This is heat!* my father boomed. The furnace was huge, with myriad ducts—aluminum tentacles—feeding each part of the house, and was a relatively simple affair to operate, once the requisite amount of coal—say, one short ton*—had been picked up in our Mazda from the lone venue in metropolitan Baltimore that still dealt in energy antiquities. The whole exercise could be readily accomplished in four or five easy trips—what with the Mazda being a two-door and all—and since we only needed to replenish our coal supply every two weeks, why, it was really quite convenient.

Starting a coal fire takes three things:

A starter—newspaper, wood—something
    to get things going
Coal (duh)
And three or four hours of obsessive
    pyromaniacal zeal

Once the jagged, glistening shards of coal (they were as shimmering as black diamonds, each with the heft and

---

*A short ton is two thousand pounds.

size of an Idaho potato) caught fire from below, something resembling warmth would, in as little as twelve hours, cast a tepid pall over the house. In order to provide even middling heat, the fire, once started, could *never go out* or the process would have to be resumed from the very beginning. It was like having a patient on igneous life support. Days and nights were consumed with "checking on The Fire," a job that fell to me, whether or not we slept there.

On the days we stayed at my grandmother's, I tried to drag Khari along with me for emotional support (or as a scrap of meat to fling toward any riotous mob, in order to effect my escape), but owing to his tender years, and undeniable adorableness, I often took pity and went it alone. I would essentially traverse the same route as if I were going to Stefan's (in case you were wondering, there was no way Stefan was going to vouchsafe his protections around the whimsical schedule of The Fire) on my commando operation. Those three blocks of taunts, hurled bricks, bottles, and insults felt like the road to Golgotha. Luckily, in the dead of winter, I was often so bundled up that my race could not be discerned; and on the few occasions that the rim of my olive skin could be spotted through the eyeholes of my ski mask, I was already inside the vestibule of The House.

Now my after-school routine of creme wafers, Chef Boyardee pastas, and syndicated television was replaced by tending The Fire and scooping the shit. Oh . . . have I neglected to mention our dog?

Oddly, though he was a Bolshevik, my father was name-brand obsessed. His manifesto was *Consumer Reports* magazine, a rolled-up copy of which accompanied him to purchase a television, circular saw, or showerhead. He wasn't interested in the absolute "best" product, but the *cheapest* item that had cracked the "best of" category, each undiscovered, no-name bargain a victory against The Man. At one point he even seriously considered purchasing a Yugo, and was deterred only by the vehicle's exorbitant cost. My father was not cheap—he was poor, with standards, an irregular fit in this world of *you get what you pay for.* He was a true snob about only a few things: jazz, the intellectual acumen of his friends, and purebred dogs. I don't think he had dogs as a child, so exactly where his affinity came from I can't say. Before we moved from Mt. Royal, there appeared a stack of *American Kennel Club* magazines.

While he had a soft spot for a few different breeds of dog, Airedales were his favorites. I think he saw something vaguely English countryside, gold four-in-hand, *lord of all one surveyed* about the handsome, stocky breed. (Remember the MG?) The dog had a stout, equable, and esoteric cachet (nobody, but nobody, had an Airedale, the distinction of ghetto favorite going instead to the German shepherd).* The summer before we moved into The

---

*It has been said that black people are afraid of dogs. In my experience in the inner city, this was generally true. I was aware of several of my white

House, we drove to the airport and picked up our AKC-registered Airedale puppy, shipped via air by breeders from Colorado. Our "training" of the puppy at the apartment on Mt. Royal consisted of reams of sodden newspapers, liberal gratuities of Milk Bones dog treats, and my father's haughty *Heel!*, which resulted in no such obeisance. As my teen years would soon attest, my father lacked the discipline required to control an animal. "Obedience classes" disintegrated into shouts, reproach, cocked-head and tongue-wagging incredulity (on the part of the dog and myself), a crescendo of tangled leashes and puppy-poop on shag carpet the sum total of his lessons. I remained emotionally removed from the process, for I knew that my father's inability to master the bitch superveniently doomed her *and* anyone gullible enough to fall in love with her.

When we moved to Madison Avenue, Koko (named for the Charlie Parker song) was nine months old and as disciplined as an epileptic lemur. It was my job to walk her thrice a day, once in the morning before school, once in the afternoon after school, and once before bedtime,

---

friends, however, who had dogs that were rabidly hostile toward blacks, the beasts straining against their chains, paws and clacking jaws jutting over the backyard fence whenever a black person walked by. The "abashed" home owner, if he was in view, would invariably *hush* the dog, or reproach, *Gilgamesh! What's gotten into you?* as the offending pedestrian hurried past. As soon as the black person was out of sight, the home owner would take the dog's face in his hands and purr, nose to nose, *That's a good dog*.

regardless of whether I was sleeping at my granny's or The House. I couldn't do it. Koko was not the kind of dog who inspired confidence, as she dragged me willy-nilly down the street, oblivious to the most rudimentary commands. The only attack she was capable of launching was upon herself, in the whirling, perpetual gnashing with which she besieged the fleas along her breeches. She was the "Charlie Brown Christmas Tree" of dogs. The secret to my survival in that neighborhood, I told myself, was inconspicuousness. Koko gathered eyes, pointed fingers, and derisive laughs wherever we went. Once she was noticed, I would be, too. This is how I decided there would be no more walks for Koko.

The House, with its discontinuous flooring and other hazards, was too dangerous for Koko to have the run of, so my father confined her to the basement, chained to a joist, where she stayed, in the dark and in the cold. After the first month, the floor became slicked with an inch-deep layer of urine and feces, which required me to tie plastic bags around my feet so I could slog into the depths to feed her, give her water, and tend The Fire. My father, not present enough to compel me to walk her, added one additional chore to my duties. Every Saturday, at the start of our "construction" cycle, I was to shovel the week's accretion of dog shit into plastic bags.

The first time I attempted to collect Koko's waste, the process was so raw and unwieldy—bits of solids and semisolids intractably adhered to the blade of the shovel, refusing to drop neatly into the plastic bag that I held open (*barely*, the opening collapsing into itself at the slightest movement or breeze)—that I nearly retched into the slop, unable to continue. Koko was no help, as she was usually so boundlessly overjoyed at the prospect of companionship that she bowed and leapt and encircled me with the length of chain, dragging me into the sewage with her, where together we howled and wept. Eventually I worked out a system, spraying whatever mounds of shit I couldn't shovel into corners with a garden hose. The stench, even after my "cleaning," was indescribable, a combination of the sickly sweet odor of death, proteinacious decay, and the olfactory singe of ammonia. After the task was completed, I swung the iron door to the furnace open to check on The Fire, adding coal to the orange and white-hot belly and shaking the spent ashes to the bottom, from where, using the same shit-encrusted shovel, I would shovel them into Glad bags already overflowing with waste.

In summer, without need of the furnace, the basement routine continued; by this point the fumes from the sweltering waste projected a hyaline methane shimmer throughout the block, as though the street were an aircraft runway warmed by discharged jet fuel. The screeching of the rats in the basement was now joined by the thick flutter of wings as bats in the chimney awoke, making sleep impossible; to this day, when I contemplate a vacation, my proximity to small mammals and working toilets outweighs any other concerns—*India for the summer? What, are you kidding me?*

The House was my full-time job by this time, and because of it, when I was twelve my friendships flagged, right when my social life was beginning to gain significance. The exception was Stefan, who came to The House often, and when asked by my father if he'd like to *pitch in*, offered, *I really don't see the point, Mr. Matthews.* Stefan would sit on a window ledge, watching my futile labors, and muse (within earshot of my father, which I loved), *You know . . . I bet I could take this place apart with my bare hands, in . . . three hours*, nodding his head assuredly before reappraising, *Maybe two.* When my father wasn't looking, Stefan would lob a half-speed roundhouse kick at a wall support or doorjamb, fairly disintegrating it in a quake of splinters and dust. *Merde*, he'd gape, *how can you live like this?* I wished I had his body for those two, maybe three hours, so that I could rent the place apart myself.

———◆———

Sometimes in that house I dreamt of the mother who had left, and of the (white) life of comfort and ease she had taken with her. The Williams sisters, and a peripheral Bolton Hill family the Wilders, were the only Jewish families I knew, so for me they were the ersatz Kahns. As rich as any other residents of that neighborhood, they seemed to me more alive, the smells from their kitchens more redolent with perfumes of excitement and comfort, their hallways graced by risky abstractions. I was drawn to them, to their oblique assimilation into the American upper class. True, the Williamses were unredeemable shrews, but their malevolence was livelier than the starched improprieties of WASPs, the professional assassins of the disenfranchised. I could see a bit of myself in these Jewish families and in the closing credits of all of my favorite television shows. I had begun to be able to discern "Jewish" names, and as a result of my obsessive TV consumption, I realized that my new heroes—Mel Brooks, Norman Lear, Austin and Irma Kalish, the two Aarons, Ruben and Spelling—were not so different in temperament from myself, all of us fancying a well-timed gag and a haughty monologue. By the time I caught a late showing of Woody Allen's *Play It Again, Sam*, I began to wonder how these people so far removed from my reality could be so close to my psyche. Surely I belonged in a luminous brownstone, or a quirky condominium, and not the slums of Baltimore? As might be expected, when reality is forced to compete with fantasy, the unknown image of my mother (who, I mused, had remarried, this time to character actor Tony Roberts, and was residing in Greenwich—either Village or Connecticut, depending upon my mood) began blurring in my mind, the hatred I felt at her leaving, and the simpatico I felt with who or what I imagined Jews to be, difficult concepts for me to reconcile. I needed an antidote to my life in the ghetto, and though I did not yet know what it would be, I reckoned that the world, and my mother, owed me as much. There was something yet, I fumed, that I could take from my mother, something she must have given me that she was powerless to rescind.

———•———

Sometimes we would stay at The House days at a time, sometimes barely once a week. My father, for all his pioneer bluster, enjoyed the creature comforts of the pull-out sofa in my grandmother's living room and her scalding showers, and was often just too tired to fight me. I took my victories where I could, and smoldered, adding to my dream of my mother one in which I tell my father how I feel about him and his world, the words at the back of my teeth like tin cups rattled against prison bars. I would not have to wait long. Five hollow-point bullets, three girls, and the dream was over.

CHAPTER IX

THE SERPENT'S TOOTH

There were three of them. Maybe ten or eleven years old, nipples swollen and straining as soon-to-be-tits loomed, asses packed like bowling balls into Chardon jeans, swathes of Johnson's Baby Powder sandwiched under their dark armpits. I had just crossed Eutaw Street on the way to The House. I saw them before they saw me. I saw everybody before they saw me; that was my job, ghetto ultrasound, street seer.

I switched the cumbrous brown paper shopping bag from my left hand to my right. I was now thirteen, but these girls had two or three inches and at least twenty pounds on me. As I passed them, still fidgeting with the bag, hoping the physical action would suggest I was too preoccupied to be fucked with, they parted around me, laughing and joking with each other, lost in their own society. I caught a whiff of cocoa butter before they were past me. I chided myself—*why did I always think the worst*—when I saw one of the girls do a 360. Like a menacing version of the Supremes, the other two tacitly turned on heel to follow their leader. I was encircled now, my eyes checking windows and doorways, as the leader, one hand raised to flatten the air in front of my concave chest, says, *White boy.*

———◆———

My Bolton Hill friends and I lived a furtive outdoor existence, basically confined to a single tiny park where we would gather every day after school or during summers to play hide-and-seek or *red-light/green-light!* Once, I tried to teach them a game Elijah had shown me called That's My Car, where participants sit on a curb streetside, the object of the game to preemptively claim the car you'd most like to possess. So, for instance, if someone spies a BMW tooling down the road before you do, and has the presence of mind to call out *That's my car!* then an endless procession of Ford Pintos or Datsun B-210s might have to be endured before there arose another shot at a decent whip. They quickly tired of this game, which they found pointless, a conclusion I came to when I spotted a Porsche Spyder rumbling toward us rather quickly, as yet unseen by my competitors, my haughty cry of *That's my car!* deflated by Paul Anderson, who corrected, *Um, that's* my *car,* as it angled into his very own driveway.

We "white" kids lived in fear of the black kids who reconnoitered Bolton Hill, like seagulls crashing into the water for prey, then flying away. Our concessions to this fear included playing our stupid games with one eye open, always aware of interlopers. If a cluster of shorn

Afros was spotted heading our way, we'd pause and hide in someone's yard or parlor until the danger had passed, and then pick the game up right where we'd left off. Racists though we all undoubtedly were, our fears were well founded. The black kids invariably beat the white kids, stole our bikes and money (I'm using a royal "us"— though I had neither bike nor money to steal, I did have bones to be broken and lips to get bloodied), and generally toyed with us until contentment or boredom set in.

Stefan found the Bolton Hill kids trifling and refused to consort with them. When he wasn't spending time with me, he hung out with the black kids from his neighborhood, but never both. As puberty neared, the *divertissements* of childhood giving way to a decidedly more "adult" predisposition, Stefan made friends with the single Hispanic kid at our school (for that matter, the single Hispanic I would ever meet in Baltimore), Hector Garcia. Hector wore a full-length duster to school, in an era when that flowing raiment suggested a pimp's sensibility and not a predilection toward disposing of one's classmates in a hail of *who's a loser now?* gunfire. A lithe, compact kid, a walking stereotype of unctuous slicked-back hair, mustache, and gold chains, Hector was a tough Colombian who spoke sleepy *we don't need no stinking badges* English. *The* pot dealer at 66, Hector was frequently spotted by the chain-link fence during recess talking to full-grown black men, the clamor of heedless children around him like so many ringing phones in an office. As the two (inarguably) toughest kids in school, Hector and Stefan were peripherally—if also charily—aware of each other's presence for most of their primary school years. That much cool could not affiliate, as cool is a one-man show. As they careened toward puberty, it became obvious to all of us at 66: Hector and Stefan, like two cats in a gunnysack, would have to fight.

The fight, when it was over, was whispered about reverentially, as though the ground had shook and the gods had wept, and no one who had witnessed it would ever be the same. In fact (even if two kids were going at it right in front of you), the words *the fight* meant the Hector and Stefan set-to—anything else was *a* fight. It was Stefan who recounted the story of The Fight to me just once, and it looked as though doing so pained him.

The time and date had been agreed upon in advance. They were evenly matched. Stefan was all training and impeccable technique, Hector hunger and feral cunning. After the first volley of blows they sprawled onto the cement, like mating pythons. Eyes were gouged, fingernails were sunk deep into windpipes. Stefan admitted, with the resigned shrug of the plane crash survivor forced to eat a passenger in order to live, that he had to bite Hector in the face. There had been no clear winner. After the fight, they were fast friends. Hector's crowd of druggies and women sated the ghetto flâneur in Stefan, who, though he was still my best friend, could hardly be bothered to play That's My Car if he was out hot-wiring one. (I kid, I think.) In the ghetto with Stefan I was safe; in Bolton Hill I was preyed upon like any other honky.

Though I never had one, bikes were a mixed blessing in Bolton Hill. Any white kid who received one for his birthday or Christmas was viewed with wistful melancholy, the unspoken sentiment, after the requisite *Man! Nice bike,* was *How long till somebody steals it?* In contrast to other cities, bikes in Baltimore were stolen not while inadequately chained to lampposts or absentmindedly left in front yards, but rather while their owners were *riding* them.

Hapless Young Whitey would be riding along, either alone or with friends. One of us, a designated lookout, was posted to maintain a visual on the streets and avenues ahead. Eleven-year-old lookouts never all that reliable, someone would become distracted by a popped wheelie or a 360, and that's when a gang of black kids, two to a bike—the extra man riding on handlebars or standing on the rear pegs—would roar through, skidding into our midst. One of the black kids would leap from his passenger position and go right up to whichever white kid was temporarily in possession of his future bike. The white kids wouldn't usually put up a fight—really, what was the point?—though on the rare occasions they did, there was plenty of rich red blood and chipped teeth to show for it. I have seen kids tossed from moving bicycles; the thieves like inner-city Comanches hanging side-saddle until the rider was felled; old men dragged from

Schwinns, bloodied and addled, simply for wandering a block in the wrong direction. Oddly, while I was rendered weak-kneed by black males (on bikes or not) I never gave a whole lot of thought to black girls.

———◆———

It had taken two or three years for Stefan to talk me into taking tae kwon do. Actually, it had taken two or three years for me to talk my father into coughing up the ten dollars a month the lessons cost, his response to my pleas an unvarying, *You wanna know the best way to fight with your feet? Run.*

My father was a big fan of avoiding trouble, not making waves.* Though he had passed his slight frame on to me, I was determined to have a say in this world, even when words failed me. Having heard (I believe on an episode of *Get Smart*) the aphorism: *A coward dies a thousand deaths, a brave man but one*, I reckoned that by my twelfth year, I was into the five figures on the mortality pari-mutuel.

———

*Much later, as I entered punk-rock postadolescence, I really wanted a tattoo(s). I had several designs picked out, as well as the artist—good friend, Baltimore tattoo legend Bill Stevenson—who would have been the perfect executor of my scarification. My father strenuously objected (not that I cared) to my getting inked, on the grounds that if I was ever wanted (by the law? the government? Interpol? he never specified) I would be *easy to pick out*. A life of crime had never entered my mind, but I guess I should have been thankful to my father for his concern about my career options.

Stefan's father taught tae kwon do classes every Saturday at a rectory on Bolton Street. (By the time we bought The House I had been taking classes for a few months; as my father never rose before eleven, doing so did not encroach on my construction duties.) There were perhaps fifteen students, most of them local kids, housewives, or students from Roye's college. The discipline demanded by this sport was staggering. It was one thing to have seen Stefan practicing the intricate patterns of kicks/punches/blocks/strikes called "forms" (*katas*), which made up the basis of the art, but it was quite another to watch as Roye expertly bifurcated the air with a snap of his leg or a thrust of his wrist, gently (but sternly) correcting, demonstrating, or praising the students. Here there was no place for my bullshit loquaciousness, quips, or circumlocutions. The body had to deliver. In the dojo, we practiced a monastic devotion to the physical world: prolonged stretching to coax truculent muscles into a burning, sensual elongation, the whole class moving as one, our bare, ordered feet slapping the wood floor in unison, the chants of the count ringing through the air, the count in which only the tenth repetition was vocalized, itself a group meditation.

We would then, as a group, assume the lotus position, from where we were instructed to meditate. Then Roye, at some arbitrary moment, would pierce the air with a slap of his hands and *we would fight*. He would pair us up by twos, and even us white belts would have to spar.* There were special pads and prophylaxes to ensure that none of us shattered a femur, or got concussed, but even with these the rectory felt to me for all the world like a Roman coliseum.

During those moments on the mat, life was in the now and in the future, offenses calculated three or four moves ahead, defenses employed extempore, our velitations the only real measure of whether one was improving or not. I suppose I was, as practicing tae kwon do required that I distance myself from the world of my father, where men ducked trouble, talked their way out of binds, *worked things out.* I was a smart-aleck, snot-nosed brat to my pop, and the truth of it was, I didn't really want to be; I pushed him because I could, when what I really wanted was for him to lift me from the ground by my collar and say, *Cut the shit.*

The girl cocked her head, never taking her hand from in front of my chest. I managed to execute the lone bit of street smarts I possessed, the ability to arch one eyebrow. That gambit had somewhat less than the desired effect. My body—drained of blood by the exertions of keeping

---

*The belt color system in the martial arts has a deceptively simple organic symbolism. The white belt—the belt of the beginner—through handling, grows darker and darker, until it becomes, ultimately, blackened.

half of my face aloft—began to buckle, my thighs turning to jelly, my knees dotting each other with denim kisses. Silently (*white boy* pretty much filling in all the backstory, character motivation, and mise-en-scène) our lean production of street theater got right down to Act 2.

I felt the inside of her elbow squeeze off my windpipe and then two sets of hands furiously burrowing into my high-water corduroy pockets. I held on to one of the two paper-rope handles on the bag, the other slipping away, tearing it. The girl's hands emerged from the bottoms of my pocket with a wad of lint and a nickel, the arm now gone from around my throat. Air rushed back in. One of them smoothed my hair. I thanked her. As I bent to collect my bag while they disbanded around me, our little drama complete except for a proper denouement, the leader, in an afterthought, turned, snatched the metal pin affixed to my shirt—"John Lennon, 1940–1980, Give Peace a Chance"(the irony not lost on me even then)— and sailed the button, discus-style, over some rooftops. Then they bopped off, laughing, the whole affair having lasted fifteen or twenty seconds. Tops.

Like Little Red Riding Hood emerging from the forest of the ghetto, I tramped back to my grandmother's house. As far as muggings go, this was relatively harmless. I was a little shaken up, but secretly elated. I now had in my possession a jewel, for which I had waited the entirety of my nascent life, and I couldn't wait to share it with my father. As I neared the apartment building, I saw him getting out of our beat-to-shit car in the parking lot. I wanted to sprint the fifty yards, but deliberately slowed my steps, drawing the beat out so that it would come neither too quickly nor too late, before, say, he began small talk, but not until he was facing me, man to man. He shut the door and with his perennially shopworn expression nodded hello.

Some niggers beat me up and took my money.

———————◆———————

I had amassed the contents of that brown paper bag, which I was carrying from my grandmother's apartment to The House, during the winter of 1980. On the morning of December 9, I awoke to the alarm clock radio playing John Lennon's "(Just like) Starting Over." As I tamped down my cowlicks and halfheartedly raked a splayed Oral-B across my teeth, Beatles songs drifted through our apartment. It must have been "Two-fer Tuesday," I reckoned, a grievously asinine programming theme dispensed by Baltimore's rock station, 98 Rock. (I rarely listened to 98 Rock, as it was the bastion of heavy metal and "classic" rock, and while I wanted to be white I certainly didn't want to be a redneck, and rednecks were the consumers of metal in Baltimore.)

When I arrived at school that morning my friend Bruno Stoller handed me a cartoon he had just drawn, which showed one stick figure shooting another stick figure, the dialogue bubble above the victim's head: *Help! I need somebody!*

I didn't get it. He snatched it back, *John Lennon was shot, Sherlock.*

Dead? I asked.

But I didn't need an answer—the elegiac programming that had awakened me, and which I now remembered, was confirmation enough. Recollecting Bruno's cartoon, the first thing I did was laugh. I laughed until hot streaming tears raced from my eyes. Kids were staring now, and this of course made me laugh even harder; I was inconsolable in my mirth, slapping my knee now and again with a *that's a good one, that's rich I'll say*. After tittering to myself like a lunatic for the first half of the morning, I spent the rest of that school day in an anesthetized fugue.

My first musical heroes besides the Beatles (Lennon) had not been musicians at all, but the egregiously lip-synching actors in the made-for-television movie *Dead Man's Curve*, an insensate melodrama that recounted in fawning, syrupy strokes the tragically short-lived career of the surf-rock duo Jan & Dean. The movie posited them as Southern California's answer to George and Ira Gershwin, their meteoric rise to the *toppermost of the poppermost* abbreviated by Jan Berry's (the Jan element) unfortunate high-speed acquainting of (his) frontal lobe with (somebody else's) rear fender. I had never heard of the group until I saw the film, but I immediately rushed to the phone as the credits ran and called my father at his desk. *Pop,* I said breathlessly, *omigod, I just heard the best music in the world . . . have you ever heard of Jan & Dean?*

In the background I could hear him giving orders to someone, discussing some inconsequential bit of the paper's operation—*Pop?! Didja hear what I said? They sing about surfing, and they have a song about skateboarding, they call that one "Sidewalk Surfing" 'cause it's like surfing, except you do it on the sidewa—*

Dave—I'm on deadline, here.

Philistine. Until I graduated to the Beatles, Jan & Dean were my favorites, and I would play their cochlea-withering crooning about girls, cars, surf cities, and little old ladies from Pasadena (about whom it was rumored that there was nobody meaner) until the record was grooveless. Wincing, my father would stick his fingers in his ears and decry, *This is not music!*

I liked rock and roll for no other reason than within the span of three minutes I could reject my father and his world, without saying a word. I had other white boys to call him nigger for me, which they did by dint of their screeching appropriation of black music and culture, repackaged into pablum digestible enough for the half-witted masses. They seemed to be winking behind their strummed guitars and molested drums, *Sorry you people couldn't make this work in any meaningful way.* That's what I was saying, at any rate.

My father's legendary stoicism, which I clumsily mimicked, made December 9 a day pregnant with grief and repression.* If I had never broken down to my father about the loss (or even the name, whereabouts, or hair color) of my mother, the murder of my favorite Liverpudlian ex-Beatle wasn't going to crack me. The admission of pain or need to another human is a transaction of sorts. The person to whom you entrust your pain has two options: to console or rebuke you. The reward of consolation not worth the risk of rebuke, at least to me anyway, I waited that day, like a dog run down by a careless driver, until I could get to a porch or dark cave and, once away from the prying eyes of others, nurse my wounds or die from them. Later at home, as soon as I turned my key in the lock, I let my book bag fall to the floor and wept, the corners of my mouth drawn to the floor as if by fishhooks, the levee strained to bursting by the day's pretensions of indifference. My father, covered in soot, hammer in hand, studied me quizzically. He said nothing, his displays of emotion at most a timorous pat on the shoulder, or a *there, there*.

Instead of inheriting a hairline that bid a hasty retreat by my early twenties or a velvet-lined box of oxidized combat medals, I received from my father an

---

*Lennon was killed at 22:49 on the evening of December 8, and, despite my owlish hours, I did not learn of the event until the morning of the ninth.

inability to feel another's pain. While I wept scalding tears for a man I did not know, they were mine nonetheless, borne out of loss. Though I could not give a name to the real losses of my life—my mother, my racial identity—Lennon (and Lennon, and the Beatles, were nothing so much as white—the Rolling Stones, with their appropriation of the blues, would have been too reasonable an obsession for me; even my father tolerated them) was a surrogate with a face and a voice. Lennon's primal screams on the song "Mother" were my own, and I wailed inwardly along with him, unable to find the lungs to do it on my own. My father was ill equipped to help speed along the ghost of my proxy. The best he could come up with was: *Imagine how you'd feel if he'd had any talent.*

It would be years before I'd forgive my father his cruelty—not for that singular remark, I was hardly that petty, but for the pervasive air of ironic detachment with which he protected himself. I was not a hustler from the corner, one of his jazz hepcat cronies, or a jaded young brother, wise beyond my years and inured to petty pinpricks and great, gashing wounds alike. For his part, he may well have been repaying me in kind for my disavowal of him; sugar for sugar, salt for salt.

Every boy must negate the person of his father, in order that his own identity might survive. I had to negate a man as well as a race, for the two were as intertwined as a tumor nestled among a bundle of nerves.

———•—•———

My father's face registered nothing. I called those girls niggers in front of him, which meant that, if indirectly, I had called him a nigger. Without taking the moment away from me, he gave me neither the satisfaction of a pained wince nor the flush of violet.

Get in the car.

We drove until we found some cops. Two white cops. They put us in the backseat, one not unkindly asking me questions, the other taking notes on a clipboard.

How many? one of them asked me.

Three.

What were they wearing?

Grey Chardon jeans.

How do you know they were Chardon jeans?

From the commercial.

Blank stares back.

You know: Ooh, I beg your Chardon.

This got a laugh, even from my dad.

Your name? one of them asked him.

Ralph Matthews, Jr.

His mother's name?

I tensed.

Even I didn't know the answer to this one.

I'm a single father.

They looked at me, and then the one with the clipboard, without really turning around, muttered, almost to himself, *Race.* There was no question mark at the end; he was probably just verbally ticking off boxes on an incident report, and "race" happened to be the next one. I started to answer, my second triumph from this minor tragedy close at hand, the *w*-sound, the beginning of the word being born on my lips when my father's voice, deep and clarion, replied, *He's black.*

The cop did a slight double take at me, then ticked off a box.

I slunk in my seat. My most recent victory in the battle against my father was a Pyrrhic one; it was his pride that would win the war that night. Despite what these gallant officers could plainly see, which was the same thing that made me prey for those girls, my father's blood had rendered me black. If only my exiled mother could have appeared at just that moment, her gentle hand staying the officer's pencil just before it blackened the "black" box on the report.

Pressed against the far side of the car, like a loveless spouse who realizes after years of marriage that the bed will never be big enough for the both of them, I didn't speak to my father all the way home. Arriving back at my grandmother's apartment building, we parked and got out of the car. Crunching wordlessly along the gravel path, my father broke the silence:

You're a nigger, too, and if you ever use that word again I'll beat you bloody.

CHAPTER X

THE STATIONS OF THE CROSS

My middle school years (ages eleven through thirteen) saw—quondam miseries I have described notwithstanding—only two noteworthy events. The first, an incipient though feckless concernment with the opposite sex; the second, the incineration of my whiteness and blackness, when, on a bright April afternoon in 1981, under a beryl sky edged with copper, I burned a cross.

———◆———

By the end of my matriculation at 66, I had amassed a whopping total of *two* "best" friends. There was of course Stefan, and then, huffing along behind in rubicund second place (I listed friends, musical groups, authors, in hierarchical order, depending on the time of day, or the arrangement of my humors), Will Lee.* Will was an old-fashioned redneck from Aspermont, Texas, where, he liked to offer, the welcome sign at the city limits read, "Nigger, don't let the sun go down on you in Aspermont."

---

*Spring of seventh grade: Musical Groups 1) The Beatles 2) The Monkees; Authors 1) Salinger 2) Dos Passos.

149

Will was one of maybe four other white kids in our seventh-grade homeroom. Another was a hollow-eyed urchin named Robert with a filthy blond crop of hair atop his flattened skull, a grubby sycophant of juvenescent drug dealer Hector Garcia. Robert spent recess with his nose jammed in a vial of a noxious and marginally illegal inhalant called "Rush," while his hands foraged below the waistband of his bedraggled Fruit of the Looms. Robert was a "dirty white boy," hopping madly about the corridors leering at formless teenyboppers—a heavy-metal iteration of the fictional characters Lenny, from the sitcom *Laverne & Shirley,* or Shakespeare's Shylock (sans Semitism). We had no idea where Robert lived (we used to speculate the congeneric locales as either a parentless shack by the railroad tracks or an outpatient sanitarium). I found his society repugnant, and steered well clear of him. Then there was Craig Harbourt, of the food stamps, who just missed inclusion into my top two tiers of friendship, victim of my certainty that there could be only two *best* friends, an oriental "whole" if you will, each friend providing what the other could not. To have added a healthy third or fourth friend would have strained my mean capacities, not to mention my sense of the "harmony" of things. My limited friendships were not entirely up to me, no matter how I rationalized the minuscule diameter of my circle. Though some kids found me funny, I knew there were but a few with whom I could spend unbridled hours without their wanting to deposit my teeth at the back of my throat. I had been told often, even by my father, that *a little* of me went *a long way.*

———◆———

A few weeks before the cross-burning, Bruno Stoller—our own Jules Pfeiffer, the author of the topical "Help! I need somebody" cartoon—had taken Will's hitherto three-year hold on second place, but we had had a falling out. Over a girl.

I was hopelessly in love with Susan Berger, a strikingly handsome girl, in the classic and unquestionably feminine sense of the word, who—for a time—even liked me back. She was in the seventh grade, but taller than I was; strong, vital, copper-haired, lily-necked, and mine, chastely, for about a week. Sexually, I was inert. I knew that I "liked" girls, but the thought of kissing them (or worse) was an odious proposition. *Someone else's spit? In my mouth?* I gagged as I thought of what was expected of me.* Television, and its two-dimensional standards of beauty (standards to which I, ironically, did not conform yet nonetheless expected from girls around me)—eyes set apart at a predetermined distance, cheekbones aloft and

---

*It is said that once a man lies, it is not so great a leap to theft, and from theft an even shorter traverse to murder; such was the journey I would make from prig to a sybarite whose face, slicked wet and ravening as a hog's in slop, in the advent of years, would have to be fairly beaten from my delectation at the split of my lovers.

chiseled, noses that neatly bisected the face without intruding—had rendered me an aesthete of the shallowest order: I loved Susan Berger because she was pretty. More meaningful allurements—her caustic wit, her compelling frankness, *Sure, we can go steady; I want a mink stole and a box of Russell Stovers*—were there in abundance behind her lineal nose and brown eyes, but they were so much haze to me, burned off by the sun of her beauty. We, at 66, called dating *going with: Will you go with me?* (the hardest words to utter to another human being, no matter the phraseology, matched only by *we need to talk*).*

I had hitherto *gone with* only one other girl, Janet Sarbanes, but I had fucked that one up royally, thanks to a very mild case of Asperger's syndrome. When Janet told me she liked me, I said nothing in return, not understanding that it was customary for the liked to himself requite endearments. I had learned from my mistakes by

---

*If you find yourself on the other end of this statement, your relationship is already dead, you are merely, as the next of kin, being notified. There is no "winning" here, and the one palliative action that will save a smidgen of your soon to be vitiated pride is simply, as soon as you hear these words, to get up and walk away. Forever. It takes real intestinal fortitude, but the lover who accomplishes this feat will sleep sooner, and less fitfully, than the passive sadsack who endures the *it's not you it's me* claptrap and *baby I can change* supplications. N.B. The get-the-fuck-up-and-get-the-fuck-out approach also works wonders for the ego when faced with *I need some space*. Move to Edinburgh: see if that's enough space for his/her ass.

the eighth grade, by which time my professions of love flowed like May sap from an elm.

Bruno Stoller was a cocky preadolescent, made insufferable by the vying ministrations of his separated parents. He lived with his mother on weekdays, his father on weekends, and within the condensation of forty-eight hours Herr Stoller attempted to etiolate Frau Stoller's place in his son's heart. Bruno was one of those kids who, in the low tide of divorce, wound up with a surfeiture of parental affections. Cruelly humored by the backslapping overindulgences of his parents, he believed himself witty, though his was a chilly, Germanic humor full of schadenfreude and pointed fingers (Bruno's mother was German, and would use irksome words like *rucksack*). For a while, the steel of Bruno's crude observational wit, forged with my own mordant drollery, made us a lethal blade cutting through the pimples and retainers of 66. But, as with any magnetized objects, once turned on each other, they repel.

I waited for Susan every day after school, during the week of our "relationship" at least, so that I could accost her with jokes, non sequiturs, fumbled professions (all of the aforementioned could and often did occur within the same sentence), *Look at me, shiny objects—don't leave dear god what does one have to do to be in your shadow or sunlight for another moment?* and this spring afternoon was no different. Outside the school I juggled and danced and

slayed woolly mammoths so that she might eat in summer and be warm in winter. As soon as my set was over,
Don't forget to tip your waitress—I'll be at the Chuckle Hut
through the fifth, I gathered Craig and Bruno around me
for the walk home. We walked on, Craig and I oblivious,
while Bruno was unusually taciturn. When we got to
Bruno's friend's house, I turned to Craig to say something or other, and it happened: Bruno kicked me square
in the ass. Hard. And then ran into the safety of his
friend's backyard. Before he got all the way through the
iron gate, Craig had nabbed him in a headlock, and was
screaming *I got him, kick his ass, I got him for you!* I listed
toward Bruno. Stopped. I couldn't do it, touching (and
tempting) though Craig's servility was. I had not yet processed the new state of things: Bruno had been my (second) best friend, and within moments, anent my
involvement with Susan, he was my enemy.

The illogic of it all stunned me. This was between Susan and myself, or Susan and him. What had *I* to do with
his feelings for her? It was I who had been betrayed. With
that thought, I felt a shudder as I foresaw the foaming,
violent rapids of girls with thin, down-covered arms and
honeysuckled musk swirling around us, and I knew then
that our only possible salvation was to hold on to each
other, as men, look out for each other above all else, lest
we be left shoaled and in pieces. This girl "thing" was not
going to go away, and if the husks of all the novels and
the spinning reels of all the movies I had inhaled were

any indication, things were only going to get worse. But Bruno, poor ninny, had been conquered, and so allowed us to be divided.

While I had always been an Omega to Stefan's Alpha—so striking was *that* contrast—among my mortal friends I was a ringleader (remember the old Warner Brothers cartoon that featured a diminutive gangster who was forever bossing around and slapping—*shaddup, Lefty!*—his leviathan henchman?) and so, with a snarling, beneficent wave, I affected Bruno's release, as though he had been a crab caught in my line and, from claw to claw, did not measure keeping. Though Susan dumped me the next day, reviled by the bruits of violence that attended our ephemeral romance, Bruno and I never spoke again. This is how it came to be that after a year on the benches, Will was pulled back into rotation.

———◆———

William Andrew Lee arrived at Mt. Royal Elementary in 1975, two years before me, and had not had an easy go if it. Will's was a real Texas twang (he claimed, with artless hauteur, to be a descendant of General Robert E. Lee; whenever his ancestor was mentioned, his eyes took on the melancholy wince of the southerner who can't quite accept that the war was over, and that they had not been victorious); and his fascination with Hitler and the Nazis I found endearingly loathsome. With his ridiculous accent, goofy bowl-cut chestnut hair, and

lumbering girth, he was a puffy marshmallow in Baltimore's steaming cup of cocoa. He had relocated from Vir-
ginia via Texas, and found himself living, for the first
time, in an all-black neighborhood. Will was singled out
immediately—mugged twice during the first five years of
our acquaintance, once at gunpoint, and both times
within shouting distance of his home. His neighborhood,
Reservoir Hill, like the projects, was well across (my) dividing line for acceptable neighborhoods, but Will's
house was really something special, almost worth the
trip. His stepfather, Peter, was a calm, laconic Vietnam
veteran, now architect, who had married Will's mother,
Lorna, in the early seventies. Peter spent most of his time
on assignment in the far reaches of the globe, his presence most keenly felt in his wife and child's lives in the
form of the copious amounts of money he funneled back
home. Interestingly, Peter's "architectural" assignments
were (respectively) in the Kingdom of Saudi Arabia, during the period of the OPEC embargo of 1979; and then in
Bogotá, Colombia, home of various and sundry cocaine
cartels, which meant that he was either a highly sought-
after swashbuckling architect or a spy, maybe both. Their
stately manse had been magnificently remodeled to in-
clude reshaped rooms, custom artwork, and brass-plated
fixtures. Twice the size of The House, it had, among the
scores of features that distinguished it from that Abad-
don, a slate landing instead of stairs and a backyard with

a garage. What a glorious prison! Will did not have the benefit of a Stefan to guide him through the ghetto, so he had to devise another means of survival.

We had all, in the collective "we" of schoolchildren and *fascisti*, nicknamed Will "The Hulk," for his predictable and predictably entertaining ability to become enraged (after some weight-related dig, "nice tits" being a staple) and lurch blindly at his tormentors, spittle frothing at the corner of his lips, arms flailing wildly, face claret and snarling—a state he could be compelled into once or a hundred times a day. His was the fissile rage of the fat kid huddled over a slice of cake, talons brandished at the world that would deprive him.

At 66, the other kids took a malicious delight in winding him up and watching him go; the game: to stay *just* outside his lumbering grasp as they teetered between hysterical laughter and giddy fear for their personal safety, as though they had pressed one of George A. Romero's zombies into service for a round of tag. I would lean against Will's shoulder while he cried and exorcised the aftershocks of rage from his body, insulting his tormentors for him until the crimson drained from his face and the streaks of drying salt cracked beneath his smiles. If Stefan was my id, Will was my unfettered anima, one who could parlay his bouts of temporary insanity into a bulwark; he knew (as evidenced in the aforementioned scabrous Robert) that black folks in general didn't want no parts of crazy. Will became sort of a tolerated curiosity in his neighborhood (and 66), and eventually kids just got bored and stopped fucking with him. But the damage had been done. He now felt like an interloper under his alabaster skin and within the gleaming oak and wrought iron of his home. Victim, pariah—Will and I were made for each other. If he had ever heard or noticed that there was something not *quite white* about me, he never let on. For my part, I let the lie my pale skin told him go unchallenged by the particulars of my family history.

Near the end of our eighth-grade year, Will and I, individually and together, were both sick of feeling like quarry. We knew that in the world outside our inner-city borders, a respect—*status*—was granted to whites that was distinctly lacking in our daily lives. Somewhere beyond the lithosphere of Dashauns, Chantes/Shawntaes, Matrells, Keisha/Lakeishas, Shavontes, Devantays, Dontays, Kenyattas, Deangelos, Lachelle/Lashae/Latonyas, the rewards of whiteness glittered like so much gold in El Dorado. The endless filmstrips we endured in social studies class, with their litany of sodden, peaceably resisting Negroes lifted high by Bull Connor's water hoses, or laid low by his rapacious German shepherds, did not represent the blacks who seemed to be in charge of the daily operations of our streets. We had yet to encounter meek, subjugated Negroes, only badass motherfuckers who would crack your cabbage for looking at them the wrong way.* Where was this mythical land where white meant power, and black meant cower? The other America, where whites were in control, banks of them holding a sea of black arms and legs and hearts in sanguinary heaps at the end of dripping truncheons—*that* was the America we had been promised in slide shows and Black History months. Barely a decade before, blacks had been dragged, beaten, and rubbed from the bottom of America's shoes for temerariously sitting at lunch counters, demanding slices of stale pie—now they were our tormentors. Something was not right; things were *out of order*. Our teachers preferred Will and me, patrolmen had either smiles or professional disinterest for us, yet we were personae non grata among the general population of urban Baltimore.† But hidden in a few frames of those hoary filmstrips, which Will and I had begun by that time to view almost as fictive, there remained one symbol with the power to hush the black students and pinch the corners of the mouths and eyes of our teachers, no matter

---

*Forced to watch *Roots* in the fourth grade, I remember Tyrone Albermarle sniggering while the teacher discussed the infamous whipping scene (*your name is Toby!* Thwack! *Kunte Kinte!*), *I wish some honky would try some Toby shit with me!*—a sentiment the class endorsed with hoots and hollers and slapped palms. While Will and a few other white kids squirmed uneasily, I pretended to feel their unease, but was also a little bit thrilled.

†This was a few years before rap music became a unifying force among all inner-city dwellers, paving the way for the cool or "down" white boy. Before that era, there were only honkies.

their race. In time, our angry whispers at the back of the class and sniggers about niggers turned to fuel, fevered daydreams and schemes to kindling.

———•◆•———

Except for his metamorphoses, Will was an amiable fellow who had to be gently cajoled into the undertaking, much as it had taken me the better part of six months to ease the word *nigger* from his lips, his southern drawl like a scabbard for that sword of a word; but lord, once freed, it tripped lightly, danced, and made up for all sorts of lost time.

We were not *complete* morons. We knew that burning a cross larger than, say, three feet in the middle of a black ghetto would be dangerous. Will's backyard (the chosen site) was plainly visible to the adjoining properties; if the cross stayed under three feet we would be safely below the sight lines, and able to avoid the inevitable full-scale race riot that would have ensued had someone seen us. The size didn't matter; it was the thought that counted. The crosses from the filmstrips might have beaten us in scope, but not in intent. I was a revolutionary. A dissident. *Nigger, don't call me whitey.*

———•◆•———

Forty years earlier, when he was the same age as me, my father had delighted in his first protest. His father, Ralph Senior, along with a Baltimore civil rights legend named either the Prophet Costoni or Tony Green (depending upon whom you asked) organized a picket line in front of the Jewish businesses of the black neighborhood between North Avenue and Howard Street in 1939. "Don't shop where you can't work" was the tag. The Prophet brought out the troops and manned the bullhorn, and my grandfather made sure they got plenty of ink in the *Afro*. Pickets like that one were a busman's holiday for Ralph Senior, whose usual protest partner was the blue-eyed blond and black Walter White, the mythic NAACP director of that time. White—passing—infiltrated the South, gathering information on lynchings and sending the information along to my grandfather and others in the black press who waited in the black parts of town, safe from the white mobs who lay for them. There were wanted posters all over the South—"Walter White— Dead or Alive," which bore no pictures of the man, as nobody knew what he looked like, and it never occurred to the racist clods that the head of the largest Negro organization in the country was every bit as fair as them. The risks for White were immeasurable, the risks for my grandfather only slightly less so.

Years after his days observing his father's demonstrations, my father had his own, somewhat celebratory foray into civil disobedience. When Fidel Castro came to Harlem in September of 1960, he wanted a meeting with Malcolm X and got one. Malcolm made sure that only three other people were in the room when they spoke: my father, a reporter from the *Amsterdam News*, and photographer Carl Nesfield. My father and Malcolm made sure that Harlem turned out en masse beneath the windows of the Hotel Theresa, one big *kiss our black asses* to Uncle Sam. Seeing that many galvanized black faces on the streets of Harlem radicalized my father, and on his return to the South a couple of years later, he hooked up with Walter Carter, CORE's Baltimore chairman. The two became a '60s iteration of the Ralph Senior and Prophet Costoni alliance, transforming the Baltimore CORE from a white-liberal, *let's all make nice* tea party to a black rabble-rousing cabal. They planned demonstrations at the Social Security Administration headquarters in Baltimore County, with Dick Gregory leading the pickets. By the time they'd negotiated a settlement, a thousand federal workers ringed the complex. This was the *first* civil rights protest by government workers, effected at one of the nation's largest federal facilities. The issues were better jobs, more blacks in supervisory positions, and comparable pay for comparable work. Every single demand was won. There were a dozen other Baltimore/D.C. protests, all fomented by my father and Walter Carter, my pop setting the players in motion, and then stepping back, pad in one hand, Leica in the other. It was my fault he missed the one he felt he most needed to be a part of; if I hadn't been only six months old, he would have been out there watching, writing—fucking cheering—as his friends Gaston Neal, H. Rap Brown, and Stokely Carmichael lobbed Molotov cocktail after cocktail, burning 14th Street in Washington to the ground in the wake of King's assassination. He never told me that when I was a kid, nor was it in any of those film-strips. It may have made a difference.

———•———

Green branches don't burn, and desiccated wood disintegrates before it can be lashed together, so we found slats of wood from the detritus of old packing crates that lined the alley behind Will's house. They would do. We bound the cross with butcher's twine swiped from Lorna's pantry, shoved the assembly into a clay flower pot, and sluiced the cross with kerosene. I had thought it would be a grandiose touch to have a torch of some kind that we could solemnly touch to the base of the cross, but Will thought that might be pushing our luck. Instead, we flicked matches in the direction of the cross from several feet away until it enkindled, slowly, an insipid blue translucent flame listlessly crawling about its right angles. Watching mutely, we were not sure exactly what to do or say. This was hardly the awesome, blazing specter of power shown on the filmstrips of draped imbeciles in backwoods swamps. The whole thing was a letdown. The preparation—the *oh my god are we actually gonna do this?*—was the event. I looked at Will, who was guiltily looking around, muttering *that's enough; let's put it out,* so afraid was he of getting caught. While the back of my throat tickled with acrid smoke and starter fluid, I watched the flame burn itself out after a couple of minutes. We couldn't be bothered to relight it.

I had tried to give a face to my hate, a black one; I had tried to give a name to it, *nigger*. The whole thing was an alembic construction: nothing had been distilled, because there was so much more to my hate, and yet not much at all. I hated the predators, who in that time and place happened to be black, a natural human response to fear. The lion hates the hyena, and beauty hates the truth,* but this was nothing compared to my fear of negation.

Despite the incendiary evidence to the contrary, I was not a racist; I was a *hater*. I hated the netherworld in which I found myself, the one that tacitly reassured me that it would shun, relegate, fear, and ignore all of me if I acknowledged half of me. Half-black, eighth-black, mulatto, quadroon, octoroon—all meant black. Do not pass go, get into jail free, don't fuck our daughters or play with our sons. I wanted to burn down Will's house, so opulently restored it was like a gold tooth in a mouth of rotting gums. I wanted to be black—charred black as pitch—so there could be no doubt; then America would have to confront me, fear me, let me revivify myself and my wounded spirit on poisoned grains; my blackness un-

---

*They are not the same, despite the conflations by mountebank postgraduate New Romantics.

equivocal, I would become a potent figure, a black-gloved fist raised in triumph at the Olympics, a menacing reminder of America's failures, a man apart, having risen from the obvious handicap of my skin, a kind of triumph in that.

These fantasies were as ephemeral as the last sputtering swirls of smoke from the dying cross. The flame was indeed out and I was still a white boy whose father had at one time been a great black man, and I was still a Jew with no mother. Those were facts as hard and vulturous as any of the girls who had mugged me or boys who had marked me. Two days later, in line behind a group of kids at the corner store, I waited for the nice old Jewish lady, Mrs. Levy, to ring them up. When I got to the register, as the last kid ambled out the door, she sighed apologetically, *Sorry hon, but you know how niggers are.*

I puked Strawberry Quik and cafeteria lunch all over her counter, unable to even nod my response, *Yes indeed, Mrs. Levy, I know how niggers are.*

CHAPTER XI

FAKING THE FUNK

George Washington Carver Vocational High School was the zoned high school for my Madison Avenue neighborhood. The name of that institution should give you an indication of its racial composition and the welcome that surely awaited me upon my matriculation. The white kids from Bolton Hill/66 either went to "merit"-based high schools, if they could support such claims, or enrolled in exurban private schools where the admission criterion was income dependent. I had no money, but what was worse, and potentially tragic, was that I had lousy grades. I had always been a middling student, the margins of my report cards filled with alternately indicting—*doesn't apply himself, attendance is spotty*—and inspiring—*obviously bright, writes well, a little more time spent on homework and he could be a straight-A student*—platitudes. Things had gotten out of hand by my final year at 66, when my friend Craig Harbourt and I skipped school for thirty-seven days—thirteen of those in a row. We always *arrived* at school during some random part of the day, but a full tour of duty was beyond our ken.

An 80 average. That's what I needed to get into the

merit-based high school of my choice, Baltimore City College High School. Every mayor or Baltimore potentate of the last millennia (or so it seemed) had gone to the "castle on a hill," as one recruiter described it, the sobriquet right in line with my own misty romantic leanings. Plus, it had the word *college* in it, which lent it a scholarly air; I could fairly see myself in its great halls, cracking recondite, leather-bound volumes or gazing broodingly from one of its windswept parapets. City had an honors, or an "A," track, which required a junior high average of 85 or above, and a "B" track, where the majority of the applicants wound up. Somewhere I had heard, or imagined, that the admissions board looked at grades only from the *first* two quarters of the eighth-grade year (the reasoning being that they had to make their decisions before spring grades were given), and so after receiving an 80 average on my December report card (and I do mean *average*—there were as many 75's as there were 85's), I absolved myself from further study, and played hooky as the leaves turned their faces to the sun. Craig and I mostly hid in the backyard of his apartment building (a block away from the school), frothing ourselves into gleeful panic as helicopters whipped the air above us, convinced that they were scouring the land for truants. At two twenty-five (the school day ended at two-thirty) we returned to the school's playground, where we leaned against the chain-link fence and waited for the suckers to egress. Kids would come out, *Where were you for Mrs.*

Jones's class? and we would look hopelessly bored (some-times, in a fit of inspiration, I would click open my switchblade, scrape the crud from under my fingernails) and sigh, *Around.*

Shockingly, I was accepted into City, and to the "A" course to boot! My pop, knowing both the wanness of my grades and the exigency of my situation, had made a call to an old friend on the board of education. My grand-mother's years in that organization had favored me, de-spite my idiocy. One call—my report card purposefully misplaced or ignored—and I was a high school freshman in the upper tier of the most academically stringent public high school in the city: I was in, and way over my head.

I had never traveled the breadth of Baltimore City on my own, and now, a slight grandma's boy, creeping to-ward four foot eight and tipping the scales at a robust (for a Bangladeshi flood victim) sixty-eight pounds, I would be making the journey to my new school via public trans-portation, commingling with adults and children, not to mention passing through neighborhoods I had hitherto assiduously avoided. Still reeling from the bloodied hole Mark David Chapman had left the prior December, an-other death rocked me, the night before my first day at City, this one much closer to home.

Elijah and I had drifted apart as he, a year older, swaggered through puberty. Already in high school for a full year, his interests had naturally wandered elsewhere. Among those he had begun to take on were the pavonine affectations of the "slick" black man, the borderline hustler; at night before bed, he would apply a tuque fashioned from a lady's nylon stocking to his pomaded head, in order to effect what he called "finger waves." His morning toilet included an endless ritual of ironing (his Lee brand jeans fit to be worn only when the pleats were as honed as a safety razor's), deodorizing/brushing/gargling/perfuming, and pruning, this last ministration in aid of the incipient mustache that vainly asserted itself above his lip (this he would also "comb" with a Lilliputian device made especially for the purpose). As a prepubescent *soi-disant* hippie, I could not be bothered with such foppery. I was clean (as clean as a thirteen-year-old boy with sporadic access to hot water and an active disinterest in the fairer sex could be) and neat, which was enough for me.

Elijah helped us at The House on weekends, but as a "brother" he had already begun receding further into the recesses of my mind. Weekends, when he would tell me lurid "high school" stories of drug deals gone awry, sexual hits and near-misses, and up-to-the-minute teenage slang, still contained fraternal warmth. The only one I can remember was the nugget (which I found unaccountably hilarious at the time): *one monkey don't stop no show*. Maybe it was his delivery.

That summer before high school, Will and his mother

had joined Peter in Barranquilla, Colombia, the locale of his latest "assignment." Will and I were supposed to have gone to City together; I viewed his departure as a betrayal, and was scarcely able to talk to him in the weeks before he left. A few weeks after Will's departure, Stefan was gone, too, but I had been through four summers of Stefan's departures, and assumed—as it turned out, incorrectly—that he would be back in twelve weeks.

I was left, then, to my books, my grandmother's bed and her television, The House, Koko (the dog), and my cats—Goldie and Calico. The prosaically named Goldie was a spunky, flaxen shorthair who explored the breadth of The House (save for the basement, Koko's domain) with mincing steps, padding across the rotted floors with the cadence of a saddlebred at half canter. His sister Calico (I called her "Callie") was black, dappled with shocking orange and russet, and was as timorous as her brother was adventurous. I loved Goldie's bravado and unconditional love, but it was in Callie's viridian eyes I felt most understood.

The back door to The House was no such presumption, just a slab of plywood, warped at the edges, admitting cold, rain, and drifts of snow that settled into corners like glacial dust. Ill-formed enough to admit all those elements, the door could not contain an adventurous cat.

On the last of those endless, friendless days in early September, I was at The House to feed the cats, shovel

the shit—the usual—when I could not find Goldie. I
searched for him until I spotted a pair of almond irises re-
flected beneath my bed. I bent and retrieved him, snug-
gling him close to my chin. As I did, he let out a wince—I
assumed I was being immoderate in my affections (they
were the only "people" I could love freely, who would
never fly off to Israel, or Colombia, or Villefranche) and
apologized with a nuzzle of my nose against his, which
was hot and dry. As soon as I let him go, he crawled back
to his hiding spot. Shit shoveled, cats loved, I returned to
the arctic central air of my grandmother's.

The black rotary phone on my grandmother's nightstand rang shortly after dinner. She sat on the side edge
of the bed with her feet touching the floor and listened
for a few moments, her lips pursed in sibilant exhalation
as though cooling a spoonful of hot consommé. *Oh heav-
ens*, she muttered, turning to me, phone to her ear, *Ralph
says the cat on the third floor . . . he thinks it's dead.* I
backed away, landing hard against the closet doors, *no,
no, no,* I begged the gods I knew not to be there. I was
still pleading when my grandmother hung up the phone
and said, *Your father will be here in a few minutes; he wants
you to meet him downstairs with some garbage bags.*

I would have refused to go. That much I am sure of.
Somehow I wound up in the car, parked in front of The
House with Elijah and my father. I know that I was
weeping when my father told me, plainly, that it was my
cat and my responsibility, and that *if I didn't go in there*

and take care of it, I *would regret it for the rest of my life.* I would have sooner put a thirty-aught-six between my legs, big toe against the trigger, the sulphurous close-set eyes of the barrel against my palate, and sneezed, than go. I remember Elijah kindly imploring me with *suggestio veri, suggestio falsi,* that Goldie was only "sleeping," and that we were "putting him to bed" for one last time. I dissolved into hysterics at his maudlin platitudes—I was well aware that cats did not sleep with their eyes open, bellies distended with gas and matted fur stuck to porous floorboards. Elijah and my dad next took off the gloves and commenced a few rounds of "tough love":

> *I ain't going. You going Elijah?*
> *Nope.*
> *Guess Goldie'll have to stay there. Doesn't seem right.*
> *He deserved better.*
> *There are things a man must— nothing in this life is easy.*
> *C'mon, Dave, I'll go with you, hold the bag.*

I sobbed myself into hyperventilation until my father stormed from the car, the bags snatched from my hands now in his. Elijah shook his head at me and followed. They took Goldie out the back door, so I never saw the plastic bag dumped into the steel cans out back.

I spent that night beside my grandmother screaming into the pillow, thinking of Goldie in the alley among the rats. It was their poison he must have consumed, and now he was food for them. Were they pulling tufts of fur from his cheeks and squealing through their bucked teeth? Was Goldie curled into a restful ball, the way kittens at sleep wrap themselves into a whirring orb of repose? Or was he stuffed into the garbage, legs akimbo, another sedimentary layer of ghetto refuse above the disposable diapers and neckbones and below the bottles of malt liquor and Roach Motels?

Without answers to those questions, I knew only that I had been born or was made into a coward, and that my father, as usual, was right that evening as he had been in all things: I had not *taken care* of Goldie at his last, and I would *regret it for the rest of my life.*

⸺◆⸺

The next day I found myself on the number 3 bus with Elijah, who attended Eastern High School (his zoned school—by that time he and Karen had moved to the "Charles Village" area of Baltimore), an okay school, which was, fortuitously, right across the street from City. They shared a bus stop, so Elijah walked me to the entrance, as he had on my first day at Adelphi Elementary nearly a decade before.

It *was* a castle, the entrance a bank of doors sheltered by a row of Georgian arches, beyond which a huge priapean tower jutted from the center of the building, in front of which was a verdant slope that dropped precipitously to the sidewalk a hundred feet below. A brusque white man, of the physical education or "shop" teacher variety, was fielding all the lost freshmen who swirled dizzily under the cupola, their hands clutching the letters detailing their class assignments. He asked them each, once, where they were going, or, depending on their level of stupefaction, merely turned over a palm and told them which way. No doubt as the result of years of stolid military movies that had insinuated themselves into my mushy lobes, I was, by the point the man looked at me, somewhat overeager as I warbled, *class nine-A, sir!* He looked at me, his face halved by the coffee mug attached to his mustachioed lips, and saluted. I earnestly half-saluted him back before he waved me away and I realized he had been kidding. I have never been able to process—in the moment—humans and their true meanings. If someone were to walk by me and say *top of the morning, fuck-bag!* I would be halfway through my *why . . . hello* before the insult registered.

In homeroom, I saw one or two faces from 66, and we nodded silently to each other like cons in the yard. The rest of my coevals were strangers. Of twenty kids, maybe twelve were black, and eight were white.* I sat in the entirety of my "back to school" wardrobe—a pair of Levi's blue jeans and an old Garanimals tunic—and watched a gaggle of voluble white kids at the rear of the class clam-

---

*That was for the "A" course, the smallest percentage of the student body; the "B" course, which comprised the bulk of City, was about 90 percent black, 10 percent white.

oring loudly among themselves.* They were talking fast, with blurring hand motions and the intimate—*Joel! No wait! Joel: Listen, in order to maintain air-speed velocity, a swallow needs to beat its wings forty-three times every second, right?*—which I imagined could only have come from years of familiarity. Before the 8:40 bell had rung, each white kid had contributed some line or another from *Monty Python and the Holy Grail.* (At the time, I had never heard of them.) So content and at home with one another were my fellow students that five minutes into their high school careers, while the rest of us bluffed or cowered our way into or from socialization, they were already settled, four years and caps and gowns but a trifling formality.

The teacher read the roll, and I kept my eyes toward the blackboard, knowing that upon hearing each name,

---

*Two days before, my father and grandmother (though it was she who usually bought my clothes) had taken me to Hutzler's department store. I prudently selected three pair of jeans, two tunics, and a woolen sweater for the coming year. At the register, the saleswoman pulled my grandmother close and whispered that her MasterCharge (it was called that in those days) was egregiously overdrawn, and that whomever was on the other end of the phone was, at that moment, instructing the store to destroy the card. Mortified, my grandmother began searching through her bag, as though a sheaf of banknotes was lurking among the folds. My dad knew that she, and we, were simply broke, so he snapped, *Ma, what are you doing; there's nothing there.* She kept rummaging, going scarlet, while the saleslady held the creditors at bay, *I don't know, Ralph.* Between the two of them, they were able to assemble twenty-seven dollars in cash, just enough for a single pair of Levi's.

my classmates would turn and stare, no doubt to select, then commit to memory, the features and quirks that would be filleted into insults or adulation over the next four years, or the alliterative, mirthfully ethnic names that would be mispronounced and misappropriated for just as long.* As my homeroom teacher—the same brusque mustachioed man from the entrance—rattled off the names of the white kids in back,

> Joel Tyberg,
> Brian Walpert,
> Avi Hirsch,
> Rachael Valentine,

a connection began to form in my brain, as the names— Messrs. Ruben, Spelling, Kalish, Pitlik—from the credits of all those TV shows that had formed the basis for my paltry understanding of the world coalesced into one big mental teleprompt and I realized: *Ohhh . . . these are Jews.*

———•———

Right around the time we moved full-time into The House (during my seventh-grade year) my identity was in such peril (my new zip code would surely, I panicked,

---

*One thing—thank you, Protestant slave owners of yore!—that I then possessed was a ridicule-free name. This would change fifteen years later when a South African minstrel and his "jam band " arrived on the scene.

belie my swollen lips and jaundiced skin) that I had begun to let slip—casually, of course, softly as in a morning
sunrise—that I was Jewish. When my friends at 66 (save
Will, who was an outcast looby, and lived so far into the
ghetto that Bolton Hill acceptance was beyond the pale
even if *he* wasn't) asked me where I was moving, I pointed
vaguely westward, or mumbled something about "gentrification," until I ran out of vagaries, their eyes clouding
over with suspicion. So I had baited and switched them.
No more Paul, I would become Saul. I tried it first with
Susan Berger, during our "courtship phase."

   As my new address edged me further into blackness
in the eyes of the Bolton Hill crowd, I thought I might assuage their dubiety (but what if it had all been in my
head? too many fevered hours spent with Poe and Tell-
tale Hearts; too many days treble-guessing the meaning
behind every arched eyebrow or harmless query) by aver-
ring, with mock horror one day, to Susan (and, fortuitously, Ann and Laura Williams, which meant that every
Jew in the school was before me), *O, Israel, And I will
pour upon the house of David, and upon the inhabitants of
Jerusalem, the spirit of grace and compassion: and they
shall look upon me, because they have mocked me, and they
shall make lamentation for him, as for a beloved friend, and
they shall grieve intensely, as for a first-born son . . .* * but
what I really did was sham a chastened expression and

---

*Zechariah 12:10—with liberties.

sheepishly confide, *you'll never believe it, Jewberger* (my nickname for her), *I'm a goddamned Jewberger, too. How do ya like that?* It had all been carefully modulated.

One afternoon I had been playing in the park with Claire Franz, Alison Gardiner, and Katie Gardiner, three winsome, budding Lolitas of Bolton Hill, and unknown to me, my father had been watching. After we had taken our harmless amusements, I left the girls and walked the fifty yards to our apartment. Leaning against his Mazda, my father bade me over.

Be careful, he said.

What? What'd I do?

He jerked his head toward the park. *Just be careful.*

Though I had an inkling of what he was driving at, to admit it would have been to admit to him that *his* reality—one forged in the black hole of some Baltimore, America, where he had not been allowed to romp and play and freely glance sweaty elbows against blond, dewy limbs—was *my* reality, and once admitted would become ever the more so, and that would not do. Infuriatingly, in a tack I knew would irk him, I made him say it, as though he were speaking Esperanto to a Hutu.

Howzat? I asked, blankly.

In a few years, when your features become a little more—look at me—when your features become a little more pronounced, and darken . . . you're not gonna be able to travel freely through that little world of yours.

Huh? I said, as though I didn't get it, or hadn't been listening.

The "Jewishness" I had asserted during my last year at Mt. Royal went untested—there weren't enough Jews in attendance to represent a discerning cultural quorum, leaving me to fudge the details with my gentile friends: *Hey, I'm as shocked by this as anyone—how do I know what Jews do on Easter?* It was the perfect shell game. I palmed my blackness, and dropped my missing mother into the con. No one, least of all me, knew what being a "Jew" was supposed to entail. How hard could it be? I'd gesture a bit more with my hands when speaking, whine a bit more (not a problem), and that would be that.

———◆———

That first day at City, surrounded by "my people," I felt a little out of my depth. I had been one of the whip-smart-aleck kids at 66, but *these* kids seemed like mini-adults, their voices raised as though conversation was a contest and whoever could pipe up the loudest was the winner. I continued to watch them, enrapt, for the rest of that first day.

I had learned some hard lessons on my first day at 66 and was determined not to suffer the same fate twice. This time, when kids wanted to know what I was, I would be primed with shot and powder, my answer locked and loaded. Sure enough, no one asked. Most of the freshmen (by the universal code of secondary school, their fraternity was limited to others of their rank) were in a stupor, trudging mechanically to one class or another, trying to figure out where the bathrooms were, whether we really had to take Latin for three of our four years (welcome to the "A" course), and sniffing peremptorily around one another's designer-denimed flanks, until the real business of high school—stratification—could begin. I was consumed with a panic that if, in this "adult" world, I did not aver my racial status it would be imposed upon me. I would have to hedge my bet.

During cafeteria—and I must pause here for a moment, and recount my wonder at the cornucopia I found in those percolating steam tables: fried chicken, meat loaf, hamburgers/cheeseburgers, macaroni and cheese, cakes and sweetmeats of every variety, a visible spectrum of Jell-Os beckoning behind sneeze guards. This was the platonic ideal of the establishment where my father, my grandmother, Khari, and myself took our annual Thanksgiving dinners, an outpost of "The Horn and Horn," where the poor and unmoored shuffled along in serpentine lines, requesting with pointed index fingers bits of upgraded Bowery fare behind glass, the feast consummated at plastic communal tables in a cheerless hall and expiated in the Horn and Horn's bathrooms, whose stalls were invariably splashed with violent, de Kooning–esque swathes of diarrhea and vomit.

I took my place at the City refectory on the edges of

a group of the Jewish wunderkinds and picked over my food. (I was unaware that my lunch tickets covered only the basics, and had had to put back—to the tittering delight and grumbling consternation of those in line behind me—my french-fried potatoes and can of grape soda, "a la carte" items, thus not federally funded.) I chewed my lunch, eavesdropping, looking for an in, a way to advertise myself.

Okay, okay, that's not—first of all—what he said, and second, I've played it—with headphones, Joel, and that's not what it says, I heard a frantic castrato voice avow. The speaker was a chubby, chalk-colored boy I recognized from homeroom, Avi Hirsch, who continued to ply his case: *Okay, okay, it says "turn me on, dead man," and then it goes—Joel—"I buried Paul" is from* Mystery Tour . . . *Jesus Christ, you're a troglodyte.* This was, I felt, an area in which I had no little expertise, so I made sure to catch his eye as he rolled his gaze beseechingly among us.

He waved me in with his narrowed eyes. *That's from the* White Album, I said, forcing a moment of deep concentration: *"I buried Paul" is from* . . . Mystery. Avi gave Joel a *so there*, and I was thenceforth included in their "Paul Is Dead" debate, which, thanks to a magazine my father had bought me, made me practically a forensic expert on the case. After a few minutes, the conversation came around to my particulars. What junior high I had attended; where I lived (now so far out of my element, I reverted to Bolton Hill as my de facto residence, which was simpler than trying to explain gentrification to this group of strangers); and then, almost imperceptibly, the night of the long knives.

And you never met her?

Nope.

I played bits of my story out tentatively, casting my line out against the surface of their questions, drawing it taut.

Wow. Dana—his mother's in Israel.

Dana's acorn eyes widened over her tuna sandwich (they always had nutritive, handcrafted meals brought from home). *Where?* she asked. I liked Dana Kargon. She was cute—a tiny Thumbelina of a girl with curly roan hair and doll features—to me, the embodiment of Leah, from *The Bronze Bow*. I could just picture her in a smart white toga with a bit of golden rope sashed around her waist.

Israel, I reaffirmed a little more loudly, assuming the child had not heard me the first time. Covering her mouth with her hand (such delicacy! at my home, we— on those rare occasions when we ate synchronously— spoke with a view of each other's medulla oblongatae, regardless of itinerant bits of ham forelegs or Gordon's fish sticks), she shook her head,

No, David . . .

(is there anything that will give wing to the beating of a young heart like the utterance of one's own name?— the lips parted wide on the *Da*, the lower lip brushed

against the teeth in a sensual bite on the *vi*, punctuated
with the dulled kiss of the tongue against the palate for
the final *d*.)

. . . where, in Israel?

Yikes.

Errr . . . near the, I think, down by the . . .

*You go to a kibbutz? I went last year, fucking sun poi-
soning, yay, thanks for the fucking bar mitzvah present,
Grandma*, Adam Lipsitz, a rangy boy with pursed lips
and wavy bangs, interrupted.

Okay. This was like chess, and so far, I'd only played
checkers. I'm trying to stay one, two moves ahead, but
they know the questions as well as the answers, and all
I've got are wringing hand gestures (cribbed from the comedian Richard Lewis, via *The Tonight Show* with
Johnny Carson) and a ghost mother. Dana is chewing her
sandwich, looking ever more disinterestedly in my direction. How do I nip this in the bud? They're comparing
bar/bat mitzvah stories now, dividing their loot—stocks,
bonds, promises of cars two years hence, international
student exchanges—like exurban pirates. Maybe they
have forgotten about me and my particulars in the
conversa— *So where'd you go to shul?* one of them asks.
The warning Klaxon in my ears has drowned them all
out—I think I heard the question, but I can't be sure. I
force an unprocessed bite of hamburger past my gag re-
flex and give them the only answer at my disposal:

Mt. Royal Middle School.

They all blink hard at me for a couple of seconds and then I think one of them sniggers, which I write off to junior high rivalry. Sis-boom-bah.

How'd you get a name like Matthews?

I will punch my way out of this wet paper bag, yet. *My mother remarried,* I say, knowing before the last syllable dribbles from my lips that I am caught.

But if you never knew her—some bright penny ventures, and then someone, mercifully, changes the subject (I think nothing of it; they have shown themselves to be a mercurial and desultory lot) and I catch my breath in the straw of my chocolate milk. A few lingering eyes sneak glances at my profile, but I feign absorption in one of my shiny new textbooks and count my dead. I figure I got off pretty easy—I answered at least one of their questions, even if it had been a softball, lobbed at me by a cretin with a cleft palate—*shul,* I tsk-tsk to myself—poor fellow is in need of a good speech therapist. By the time I finish my sandwich, I'm feeling rather optimistic about my social chances. The contretemps hadn't lasted nearly as long as my inquisition at Mt. Royal—owing no doubt to my matured powers of dissemblance—and if I was not mistaken, I had ingratiated myself into their society quite nicely. We all finish our meals, and though I do not reenter the gravity of their planets for the rest of the cafeteria period, I am not worried. This would work for me here, as it had worked for me at 66, as it would work for me always. There was nothing more to Jewishness

than to whiteness after all—it was no different than saying one was one-quarter French, a little bit German, and
a smidgen Danish.*

Right?

Filing out of the cafeteria, I was buried a few bodies
behind my new "chosen" people, when I heard Avi
Hirsch say to Joel Tyberg, *Jewish, yeah right—who's his
mother been fucking?*

———— • ————

My first six months at City passed without major incident. I was alone, as I had never been before. Stefan,
my social Cerberus and all around wheel-greaser, did not
return from summer vacation. My only companionship
was my daily after-school walk across the street to Eastern High School where I would meet Elijah for the trek
to the bus stop. Sometimes we would take a roundabout
route, and stop off to play Galaga or eat an oily bag of
french fries (these diversions usually took place within
the same establishment).

At City, I was no longer "the smart one," as I had
been at 66. The most dim-witted of them had read more,
seen more, done more than me. The boys bewildered me,
with their Dylan circa *Highway 61 Revisited* manes, their
pretensions and petulant sense of entitlement, and the

---

*I am still unaccountably infuriated by such assertions by whites. Unless
you have direct, palpable relations in these countries, and/or can speak
Dutch/German/French, you are merely white. Enjoy.

girls beguiled me, with their stormy eyes and awkwardly beautiful features. I spoke to the Jewish kids more than I spoke to anyone else at City, which was not very much, and continued to try to puncture the wall of their society like a dogged spermatozoa. Often on the way to the bus stop after school, I was glum, and when Elijah asked me what was wrong, I would confide in him that none of the kids I liked wanted to be my friend.* He would answer, with a fist pounded into an empty palm, *Fuck them peckerwoods*, and I would laugh.

After bouncing from apartment to apartment, he and Karen moved into a two-bedroom place in Bolton Hill, sharing a bedroom let to them by a single black man named Larry. At the time, I found it odd that a single man would share his apartment with a mother and son, but there was in all likelihood much more to the story than I was aware.

Larry was a wiry, silent man of thirty, with jet-black features and a mustache the envy of any highway patrolman. He and Elijah got along cordially, the territorial posturing of two black men at various stages of potency (with a single white woman thrown in for a dollop of frisson) amounting to little more than tacit détente. One evening, Elijah and I had stayed out well past curfew playing Ms. Pac Man at an all-night diner, and on the walk back to my grandmother's apartment building, we

---

*I was not made of much.

noticed my father's car under the driveway's canopy. When we walked up, my father was just coming out of the high-rise's double doors. Wordlessly he drew back his forearm, smashed me across the neck, and said to Elijah, *Get in the car.*

Hours later, my father came back to my grand-mother's alone, and told me that Larry had beaten Karen, and that he had taken Elijah with him in order to prevent the boy from taking his revenge. My father was prescient in these matters, as the very next day Elijah vowed to me that Larry would be dead before the new moon. Ultimately, Larry was not arrested, and Elijah's plan for revenge was frustrated by Karen's decision to flee with Elijah to San Francisco three days after the attack.

School then became a prison for me and, fittingly, routine was my only comfort. The one person who was fixedly present—save my father, who was always at work—was my grandmother. She, Luke, Laura, Robert Scorpio, and Anna Devane were my hearth.

My grandmother and I had gotten strung out on the daytime television serial *General Hospital.* I won't recap the "plot" of this asinine simulacrum of what middle-aged, alcoholic Hollywood writers imagined life to resemble once logic had been replaced by id; suffice to say that it contained elements of science fiction, international intrigue, and creepy psychopathology efficiently ladled down the gullets of housewives (and the odd schoolboy) every weekday between three and four in the afternoon.

We were then in the grips of the cultural phenomenon known as "Luke and Laura," which, for those not old enough to remember, or who prefer to forget, was a national idée fixe involving two insipid characters: Luke, played by an obvious homosexual with a sparsely permed flaxen mane, and the subject of his *l'amour fou*, Laura, portrayed by a sexless, flat-chested blonde fresh from musical theater. Luke had, after a lifetime (in soap opera time, about three earth weeks) of unrequited love for Laura, decided that the most efficacious way to demonstrate his tendresse for the prude (who had gone and followed her meretricious little heart by marrying a lawyer named Scottie Baldwin, a stalwart member of the community) was to patiently, if also decisively, one klieg-lit evening, rape her. I was enough of a budding sadist to relish this fantastical, sanitized bit of sanctioned cruelty and had surmised that Luke was just an ebullient romantic whose ardors could not be bound by the continence that governed less visionary sorts. I smelled subversion in the story, and in a feat of sociopathic legerdemain, the writers, concerting all of their powers, had made Laura the villain (!) for her implacable animus toward the man who had loved her enough to reveal the depth of his passions.

I was in heaven and my grandmother and I cheered, jeered, and swooned as Luke went from predatory cur to gallant knight, scarcely before his lover's torn labia had healed. Since this dramaturgical adventure relied on cliffhangers to shepherd viewers through its untenable plots, it was imperative that if I wished to enjoy the resolution of the previous day's scandals, I must arrive home as close to the beginning of the episode as possible. Trouble was, City was ten or fifteen miles from home, and did not let out until 2:30. *General Hospital* started at 3:00.

Each day in seventh-period Latin class, I stared at the clock, my book bag gathered in my hand like a riding crop, the final bell the gate. At the sound, I slid through the lingering, socializing youths as effortlessly as O. J. Simpson through an airport lobby, and was free of the school doors by 2:32. If I timed it fortuitously, I was on the number 3 bus by 2:38 (the descent down the mountain was not something one could do both elegantly *and* hurriedly, and I was my father's son); after a ten-minute ride, and transfer to the number 8 bus (which, if I was lucky enough, I could catch by 2:52), I could feasibly make it home by 3:16 or so. Once or twice, all the gods aligned, the bells, hallways, bus stops cosmically synchronized, and I managed the hat trick of a 3:02 arrival.

At this point, the edges of my grandmother's mind were clouding over. While we sat together and watched television, names would sometimes escape her so she'd refer to characters by their primary characteristics. Luke, for instance, began as *That Rascal*, only to evolve into *The Good One*, as in: *Davy, what happened? Why'd she do that?* My reply: *No, Grandma, she's on his side, you know . . . The Good One.* She'd recline a bit in her chair and sigh contentedly, *Oh, him . . . I like him.*

For nighttime television comedies, the degree of her favorite character's craziness was the most important arbiter of a show's merits. Sometimes she would remember the character John Ritter played (on the sitcom *Three's Company*) and exclaim, *Oh good, Jack is on!* At other times, she would stare at the TV blankly while Mr. Ritter mugged and bumbled through the Molière-via–Santa Monica sitcom plot, and ask, *What's this?* I would say, *You know—Jack, the two girls . . .* and her irises would snap back into focus, *Ohh, he's crazy.* Her world of Jack Trippers, George Jeffersons, and Hawkeye Pierces made her own tenuous grasp on the moment bearable. Often she called me Ralph, which did not bother me; I was honored to be mistaken for her only child—not such a painful second place to be in.

By the end of my freshman year, the exertions required to make it home by the opening credits of *General Hospital* had proved too great. It seemed to me that a fair portion of my arrival time could be shaved off if I never departed. So, as my days staying at my grandmother's grew more frequent (even my father recognized the difficulties of studying, eating, and being a high school student amid the privations of The House), I would walk out of her apartment bright and early each morning, hide in the concrete stairwell that abutted our unit, listen for

the hacking cough and jangle of keys that harkened my
father's departure for work, and after perhaps another
fifteen minutes (in order to allow for forgotten documents
or misplaced car keys) would ring my grandmother's
doorbell. I'd breeze in, offering up a blasé, *missed the bus*
or some halfhearted prevarication (after the first week I
stopped explaining, and she, with a pained squint,
stopped asking), and would plop down on the couch for
the rest of the day. My grandmother was not happy about
these arrangements, and it was a testament to her benef-
icence as well as her encroaching senility that she never
told me to get up off my ass and get to school.

After that first year, I had a solid D-average.

There were not many Jews in the "B" course. The B
course was mostly black (as was the school), with a few
working-class, almost-achieving whites salting the ranks.
The B-course students, who were not as manically consumed with one-upping each other as the A-course kids
were, were happily average. As much as the Jewish kids
reminded me of me, it was a halcyon, idealized, fictive
me, one who had been kept close to my mother's breast,
treated to years of orthodonture, cable TV (so that I, too,
could have absorbed the lessons of *Monty Python*), and
kibbutzim.

I continued to snooze through my classes at City to

the consternation of many caring and not altogether un-skilled teachers. My favorite English teacher, Mr. Rosskopf—a woolly, bearded ex-hippie—played us Cre-taceous rock albums in an attempt to teach us the sub-tleties of simile, metaphor, and allegory. We listened to Dylan's "A Hard Rain's A-Gonna Fall" and "It's All Over Now, Baby Blue," both of which I found inscrutable. I did find it odd that amid a class full of black children, Mr. Rosskopf trotted out musical examples as culturally sig-nificant as surfboards to Aleutians.

My social studies teacher, Mr. Cornell, was a serious, very dark-skinned cat with an Afro, a brother pining for the revolution that never was. He rarely smiled, though when he did it was the knowing, cruel smile of the peren-nially disappointed. I knew, from my rear perch in social studies class, that Mr. Cornell's heart had been broken, and that black people had done it. Whenever a white kid would raise his hand to answer a question, Mr. Cornell would scan the room, his eyes soliciting every averted brown gaze and doodling caramel fist, ignoring the white kid's hand for an imperceptible beat.

I had as much riding on those black hands as he did. I recall those many months in Mr. Rosskopf's class, snooz-ing fitfully, or surreptitiously inhaling the contents of the John Dos Passos or Ross Macdonald paperbacks hidden behind my textbook. I'd raise my hand with the frequency of a lunar eclipse, but when I did I would be wryly dis-missed with *not you—I know you know*, and a call for other volunteers. *Oh yeah? How is it that you know that I know, Mr. Rosskopf?—I got straight D's all last year, barely—if, in fact, I did—passed the ninth grade. All those quizzes of yours I've flunked? My witty banter while you're at the blackboard?*

Between what Mr. Rosskopf knew and Mr. Cornell's pause was the history of my passing. The best would continue to be assumed of me, even as I demonstrated the worst. The game had been rigged; had Mr. Cornell not introduced that pause, which was as enfeebling as the most robust pity always is, I may not have internalized the notion that being black meant that you could compete equally with the best and the brightest, as long as the world gave you a couple seconds' head start. Had Mr. Rosskopf not been so smugly dismissive, I might have ventured out into the world where nothing whatsoever was expected of me, and chosen to fail, or not, on my own. I would go on to become quite the failure, but when you're white, failure is a tragedy; when you're black, it's a statistic.

The autumn months of the tenth grade saw me scuttling along the baseboards of City, unnoticed yet acutely aware of all that played out around me. I watched freshman girls dancing atop the insinuating fingers of senior boys in abandoned hallways; I watched teachers suck the marrow from cigarettes in the parking lot between classes, commiserating like department-store Santas or off-duty cops (which, I suppose, they were). I was rarely where I was supposed to be, and I was such a nonpresence in any event that I was never missed. I often took extended lunch periods, remaining in the library for all three cafeteria sessions. There was a game I played with myself, wherein I would see how many hours in the school day could elapse without my having uttered a single word to anyone. I read everything I could pry from City's well-stocked library shelves: *The Hagakure; The Mill on the Floss; Paris Spleen; The Idiot;* Iceberg Slim; *A Good Man Is Hard to Find; Tales of the Uncanny and Supernatural; Smoky; Typee* (and *Omoo*); *Raise High the Roof Beam, Carpenters and Seymour: An Introduction; Let's Hear It for the Deaf Man; The Yellow Wallpaper; Looking for Mr. Goodbar; Working and Thinking on the Waterfront; The Digger's Game; Confessions of Felix Krull, Confidence Man; Spring Torrents; Notes from Underground; Flee the Angry Strangers* . . . and comprehended little, all before Christmas. Along with a novel every two to four days, I juggled a daily brimming plate of television and a demitasse of schoolwork. There were no pesky friends, girlfriends (still no short and curlies, voice changes, or growth spurts!), or extracurricular activities (save the scurrying to and fro The House for demolition/sanitation) to divert me from my escapism. I didn't miss people at all. I didn't miss friends. One day was as the next in school, until one day was different.

I was in a social studies class (I cannot remember

what the subject matter was, but I do know that one of my exams contained the query: "What is the function of the Diet in Japanese government?" and I promptly filled two pages on the importance of elected officials' consumption of a proper ratio of legumes, fruits, and grains in order to effectuate proper governance), half-dozing, when I heard a violent motion of chairs and desks behind me, accompanied by a great scuffling of bodies. Alarmed, I turned in my seat and saw seven or eight girls standing breathlessly around the lone, unoccupied desk, an archipelago amid their sea. Best to determine, I wondered, exactly what it was about *this* desk that had inspired such a frenzy. Solid surface . . . no more nor less marred than any other desk in the classroom . . . legs all touched the floor . . . maybe it was the chair—and then I happened to glance where they were looking toward the front of the class. I watched one of the girls stutter, *sit here*, and then, like summer hail, the others clamored against Mr. Freeman's

Will you please sit down! with

No! Sit by me! The contested desk screeched hither and yon, before finally being offered up to the hewn from marble deity who stood, a gentle smirk upon the alpenglow of his features, at the head of the room. Of course, the proffered seat went politely untaken, to female murmurs of *shit, you fine*, and *goddamn!* and Stefan came and sat right next to me.

The years had been kind to Mr. Templeton. Gone was

the hesternal baby fat, replaced by coiled, sinewy muscles; his European garments adhered obscenely around
his body. Apparently, the last year and a half spent skip-
ping puberty had landed him into Olympian godhood.
The vagaries of international academic transcripts being
what they were, Stefan was temporarily placed into the
"B" course. Much to the jheri-curl wrenching dismay of
all the "B" girls, and owing to Stefan's natural intellect,
his enrollment in the A course was delayed no more than
a month.

Stefan's lethality, as it extended to the fairer sex, is
impossible to overstate. Girls quite literally fought each
other in a whirl of fingernails and pulled earrings for his
attentions. For the record, most of the (American) girls
who toppled astern were black. White girls looked but for
the most part did not dare act upon their avidity. I
watched, bemused, sickened, shot through with envy as
a group of ten or fifteen private school (white) girls accosted us (who am I kidding?—*him*) one day in Bolton
Hill. They circled, each one daring the others to touch
him, until one, overcome with venturesome ardor, tore a
page from one of her textbooks and asked, with trem-
bling hands, if she could wipe the sweat from his brow, in
order to have even an ephemeral bit of him. He laughed,
but did not refuse (a gentleman to the last!), and she did
so; when she had finished, she stood staring at the page,
hissing with territorial menace as her friends tried to

touch it. I used to imagine the girl with half her fist or an abused Claussen dill stuffed inside her, Stefan's pheromone swatch jammed against her nose like an oxygen mask.

With the volatile addition of sexuality to our friendship, traveling in Stefan's shadow became increasingly stultifying. I was Pete Best, John Oates, Peter fucking Lawford. I hated him, as any normal, venal, self-absorbed orphan would have; and I loved him still.

No longer anonymous, I was now part of an entourage, an unwilling male sycophant in a sea of pliant women. This required my adopting a peculiar rhythm of speech when walking down the street with Stefan. We'd be bopping along, shooting the shit, when I would spot a girl or girls somewhere ahead of us. As we neared, I would simply stop talking, wait for the ineluctable peals or blatant stares that discomfited me with their frank invitations for him to do whatever he liked to their downy flesh and yawing thighs. I looked away, or at my feet, for I knew that I did not rate even his runoff, and I spent days in front of the mirror in my grandmother's medicine chest, wondering what it was about the aggregation of my features that rendered me invisible. Stefan took the attentions lobbed his way as his due, but "girls" didn't really interest him all that much; he had already fucked countless lissome seductresses in C'ap D'ail. He could not suffer the marathon make-out sessions with

American teenyboppers, the interminable assault their virginity required before prudery—their sexual default—sentenced one to chafed lips and wracked testicles. No, he aimed his fifteen-year-old phallic trebuchet at the college coed/divorcée/cocktail waitress set. Ignoring for a moment the fact that I still didn't know a Volvo from a vulva, let's broach, as soberly as possible, the object—the word *subject* doesn't quite apply—of Stefan's cock.

Obviously, I never witnessed his manhood in any condition other than somnolent repose; but inert and flaccid, it swung like a limbless iguana, all brown mass and gravitational pull toward the floor, at about nine inches as the crow flies. It was uncircumcised, which only added to its mystique, as though the attending physician had, upon wielding the scalpel after his birth, somberly declined to prune a work so divinely inspired.* His wardrobe was filled with tailored shirts that highlighted macho décolletage, kid leather half-boots, and pants salaciously plastered around his haunches. There, in the forward "V," plainly visible, was the outline of his superior breeding. Women and men's eyes were drawn there, sending a vermeil army to their cheeks. There were jealousies, and envious cabals among the more "street" lads at school, who didn't *know who that nigger thought he* was;

---

*I know now, of course, that Stefan was born in Europe, and they are just icky that way.

but not much came of it—how do you rail against the sun, or the moon, or God?

I was fifteen before my body belatedly decided to poison me with the gift of semen. Asleep next to my grandmother, I awoke one night suddenly, vaguely nauseated. I lurched to the bathroom, unsure of whether I was going to be sick or not, when I had the presence of mind to check the inside of my briefs. There was a sheen of glutinous clear fluid, and I realized that I was not sick per se, but rather . . . *disquieted.* I gave the situation no more thought and went back to bed.

Around this time, there was something in Baltimore called "Super TV," a precursor to cable television. For a monthly pittance you could enjoy second-run theatrical movies from 6 P.M. until midnight, and thereafter vigorous pornography. My family could not afford such luxuries, but all was not lost. A few weeks after my nocturnal intermission in the lavatory, perched in front of the television in the living room, I endeavored to tune in Super TV. How could I watch Super TV when we were not subscribers? The answer depends on one's definition of "watch," as I could, thanks to a Job-like patience, make out—every three or four minutes—a flash of recognizable images, albeit in negative form, as the scrambled picture briefly aligned. It was like timing the entry into an alternate dimension. I did not understand why I was watching the squiggly, intermittent shapes that undulated like some erotic lava lamp, but my cock was, for some reason, in my open fist, and I could not seem to stop. My first or-gasm was attended by a fearfully whispered, *What's hap-pening to me?*

With Stefan in my life, of course, there would be no girls for my delectation. Sexual maturity nonetheless awakened feelings of need in me I had not felt since the days of Jan. With the advent of my interest in girls, the hole my mother had left me proved infinite. Now that de-sire was merged with want, I became a feckless masher of *Young Werther*–like proportions, my specialty twenty-page, tear-stained billets-doux. I fancied myself a ro-mantic hero on craggy windswept cliffs, fjords foaming and frothing below, the girl of my dreams snuggled against my chest. Having had no real feminine presence in my life, I viewed girls as objects to be acquired, the ac-quisition of whom would prove to me whether I was worth . . . anything.

There was one truly beautiful girl in my school, Lisa Hodges, a copper-colored black junior with an effort-lessly pursed mouth and skin as smooth as a shaved peach. She was brilliant, and from a somewhat "Huxtable-esque" suburban family—Mom was a nurse; Dad was a lawyer. Though I did not tell anyone I was black, I would have permed my hair into jheri curls and dusted off my dashiki for one kiss from her. Lisa waved me to her locker one day when Stefan and I were walking down the hallway between classes. I may have actually pointed at myself, then back at her to make sure I hadn't been mistaken. Instead of waiting, she walked right up to me and whispered, *You have the most beautiful green eyes*, and, with the brush of her hand against my cheek, walked away. I stood, wonderstruck, until my reverie was interrupted by Stefan putting an arm around my shoulder exclaiming, *That's my motherfucking man!* I replayed her words, and the fifty amperes her fingers had charged against my cheeks, a thousand times that weekend. Someone had seen some kind of beauty in me, which I had assumed was as grey and nebulous as my identity. By Monday, I had contrived (by not going to class until my plan was effected) to "bump into" Lisa by her locker. I walked up, a bucket of sand crabs in my belly, and said *hi*. After that, I reckoned, the words would come, punctuated by the sweetly awkward exchange of telephone numbers, tentative plans—movies . . . the mall?—and finally the verdancy of young love. She said *hi*, and a wave of tenderness crashed over her features. *I have to, you know, stop you before you start . . . I just did that to make Stefan jealous.* And with that, she laid those same fingertips against my bony shoulder, and walked away. *You do have nice eyes, though,* she added, over her shoulder.

There would be other nugatory high school "romances," but that hand against my cheek was pretty much the extent of my teenage sex life; thereafter, I had to content myself to jerking off to Stefan's conquests, the pudenda storm of glances, licked lips, and twirled hair that rained upon him.

———◆◆———

Stefan's celebrity at City was such that even the Jewish A-course kids included him—and if only by extension me—into their circle. They didn't seem to care about Stefan's racial background; his European credentials rendered him more exotica than threat to their women and valuables. Stefan was so sure of the rightness of his view of the world, specifically the parochial "faddishness" of racism in America, that he genuinely believed it no longer existed, a belief commonly held by those who have never indulged in or suffered from it. This was how, or why, Stefan never looked past the nether regions of his chin to notice that I was passing, which I'm sure would have bemused and horrified him. With Stefan's imprimatur, the Jewish kids accepted me as some kind of an oddity, a Jew by dint of the fact that I wasn't technically *not Jewish*. I alternately explained my father away as white, Lebanese (I read that Jamie Farr, Klinger from *M*A*S*H*, was Lebanese), or Palestinian—basically any swarthy peoples about which little enough was known so that my lie could be neither verified nor refuted with any exactitude. In retrospect, the Palestinian ruse was an unintentionally inspired bit of subterfuge. Pairing my Jewish mother with an Arab was only slightly more fantastical than her marriage to my father.

Luckily for me, nobody then paid much attention to the differences between Middle Eastern cultures. The love affair I fashioned between my Palestinian father and Israeli mother was a short-lived coupling among the sand dunes that resulted in my birth. In my imagination, my mother had undergone a transformation to a full-fledged Israeli. I needed to break out the big guns in order to quell the suspicions of my Jewish friends, and Israeli seemed like a Jew squared: *I'll see your Jew and raise you an Israeli.* The kids seemed to shrug off my explanations of the day, but on occasion I trotted out the Palestinian bit to their parents, and detected scowls and arched eyebrows in turn. That was the look I dreaded, the one I assumed would greet me had I told anyone I was black. I couldn't have known—without cracking a history book, or reading a newspaper, chores I could hardly be bothered with—that my assertion of Arab descent was every bit as loathsome to my friends' parents as my hidden blackness.

The wheels greased by Stefan's popularity, I made a few more friends, and even became a regular at some of the Jewish kids' houses, taking easily to their carpeted dens and stuffed pantries. At *my* home, food was purchased on the day it was to be consumed and nothing was cooked *á la minute*; instead glacial plastic bags were submerged in roiling water until heated through, or tin cylinders of "pasta" were upended into skillets for smelting. Without vegetables, butchered meats, or fresh seafood, the closest thing to a prepared meal I can recall was the assemblage of a dish of ground chuck coated with brown treacle, "Manwiches," which deadened the taste buds and quickened the heart rate. We had gone on food stamps by my sophomore year, and I withered from shame during my daily trips to the A&P supermarket. All the check-out ladies recognized me from the times I used to come with my grandmother, but her health had declined over the last several years to the point that I was now in charge of hunting and gathering. I would force Khari to go with me and, after we selected our day's rations, would leave him in the checkout line to remit the government-provided diktat. I waited outside around the corner, and when I met up with him again out front would ask, *How'd it go?* He would answer, quite cheerfully, *Great!* as though there was nothing extraordinary or shameful in the dégringolade of an American family during the Reagan era. I really marvel at who I must have thought I was.

The kitchens of my Jewish friends had walk-in pantries lined floor to ceiling with snack items. They would stand in front of their two-doored fridges, sullenly poke its teeming shelves, and then complain to their moms that *there's never anything to eat around here.* Try as I might to adopt the same disaffected attitude, my mouth watered and my heart coveted. I stood with them on the lawns of their homes as sixteenth birthdays arrived, heralded by new, or gently used (usually Bavarian), coupes, wrapped in garish ribbons and attended by girlish squeals or scarcely convincing *no wayyy*s.

Knowing nothing of shtetls, holocausts, or pogroms, I equated Jewish with money and smarts. The WASPs from Bolton Hill had been smart, to be certain, but their intelligence was benign, an acuity best employed, for instance, in understanding how photosynthesis occurred, rather than the deceptively simpler but more profound reasoning as to why ketchup does not belong on a hot dog. Jews were cool, and I shared *something* with them.

The first thing these parents—usually the father—would ask me upon making my acquaintance, often during our salutary handshake, was, *What's your nationality?* There was never a time when this question was delayed more than five minutes. Because I was often a potential suitor for their daughters, the need for them to be made to feel at ease was even greater. Their fear of me, and my desire for their acceptance, were the final nails in the coffin of what little was left of my public blackness. I would have written their inquiries off as inoffensive cultural curiosity were it not for the fact that in Baltimore there were no "nationalities" save black or white. The question was a not so coded inquiry into my race and once I had given a satisfactory answer, i.e., white (Jewish), I was treated to their ruminations on how the

*shva*s (short for *schvartze*s, the Yiddish equivalent of niggers) were ruining the city.* No one nodded along more
vigorously than I.

———————◆———————

Every once in a while, there would be an announcement over City's P.A. system regrettably informing us
that *so and so* student had been shot to death the night
or weekend before. Girls would gasp, and occasionally
run from the room, and some of the boys would shake
their heads and brush at the saline that rushed to their
eyes, or simply whisper *goddamn* to each other, heads
bent close. The victims were always black boys. I rarely
knew them, but could occasionally put a smooth, shadowy face to the name, and add them to the list of ancient
dead, golden cats, and former Beatles I had hardened
my heart against. After one such announcement, when
my ruth had clung to me like napalm, we watched the
Holocaust documentary *Night and Fog* in Mr. Petr's
English class. Mr. Petr, a City legend, was in his sixties
and wore his white hair and trimmed beard in the style
of "Papa" Hemingway, and true to form liked to trot
out his war stories with gusto. He had been in Korea

———————

*There is the possibility that many whites throughout my life were
somehow aware that I was mixed, and simply remained silent on that
score, while unguardedly voicing their general racism in my presence.
That is an unlikely (though horrifying) possibility, the ramifications beyond my ken.

and killed a man, and took righteous pride in telling us he had retched as soon as he had pulled the trigger. Mr. Petr was from old Baltimore, bred of Polish blue-collar stock, and had lurched into teaching via the GI Bill. He was tough, and swore freely, and should any young "punks" get out of hand was rumored to be handy with his fists. (We were not that kind of school, but I did watch him give the bum's rush to many recalcitrant boys.) He could not be bothered with political correctness (though no such presumption existed at the time, thank god), and addressed his students with improvised nicknames, which were usually malapropisms of our actual names, admixed with some comment or rhyme pertinent to our ethnicity, sexuality, or hygiene. Thus, young Kathleen Poteat, a coarse, vaguely redneck girl with feathered hair and an accent forged in the steelyards, became *Miss Susie Rottencrotch*; Stefan was *Dandy Randy* (for some reason, in official capacities, Stefan was known by his Christian name Randall); and to my boundless delight, I was *Little Herman Finklebaum* (or Myron Flunkleman, or some such other Brighton Beach–toned invention), which meant that this old, irascible racist considered me a Jew, based only on the evidence of his eyes. That was the plan, after all. As Alain Resnais voiced-over grainy images of skin-wrapped corpses being dumped into ditches, or clinging to chicken wire with skeletal fingers and haunted eyes, Zelda Gessen—a beefy Jewish girl—got to her feet and made for the door. Mr. Petr boomed, *Where the hell do you think you're going?*

Those are my people! she shrieked, tears dripping from her chin.

On your ass! Mr. Petr commanded, pointing the way back to her chair.

Zelda choked out another sob and ran from the room, Mr. Petr in hot pursuit. I could hear his raised voice out in the hall. For some reason, I hated Zelda at that moment, and wished that her carcass would be flung into an incinerator, her fat rendered into soap, her hair spun into carpet. While I was sickened by the footage of those long-ago events, here at City a fellow we had all—at least proximately—known was barely twelve hours dead. Where were her righteous tears for him? This boy had also been *one of her people.* Her words echoed in my head, a bitter echo of the excuse my father had given me for my mother's departure—she had *gone to fight for her people.*

What was it about Jews and *their people* that superseded their general alliance with the whole of humanity? Their holocaust, to be frank, paled in comparison to the ongoing deaths—physical, economic, and psychic—suffered by my other people. I hated Zelda for her insular pity, and Jews for their "trump card" of the Holocaust. I reckoned that six million people gassed and tortured and murdered was a small price to pay for a nation to call their own, carte blanche on victimhood, and a poverty rate of less than 4 percent. The way I figured it, they got off easy.*

I had heard the gunshots—a riot of scattered *pop! pop! pop!* followed by screams or, more ominously, pallid silence, and a strobe of flashing lights and dinning of sirens—often from the direction of the Bruce Manor Projects (which lay just a couple hundred yards outside my bedroom window at The House) on many occasions. What had happened, over the course of the first few years of the eighties, was crack cocaine and Ronald Reagan. These two forces aligned (*allied*, my father would avow) to make the inner cities a world of smash and grab, seek and destroy, duck and cover. Success, or the symbols of success in trickle-down America, had morphed from preppy, name-brand excess (Polo, Izod, Benetton) into the inner-city black American approximation of wealth, attended by the coveting of College Basketball Windbreakers (schools neither played for nor attended), Leather/Lamb Outerwear, Gold Chains, and (still) Nike Basketball shoes. None of these items signifying a young black man's grandee was cheap. They required money in an era when education, despite the laugh-tracked moralizing intimations of Mr. "Heathcliff" Cosby, was no guarantor of the success that might most reliably, legally, and

---

*In *American Holocaust* (New York: Oxford University Press, 1992), David Stannard estimates that some 30 to 60 million Africans died being enslaved.

meritoriously bring it. I saw kids wear a pair of beat-up Converses to school, which, once inside, would be replaced by a secreted pair of Nike high-tops or suede Ponys. You could literally be shot for your clothing, a fact that most of those crackling death notices blaring over the intercom bore out. Stefan, despite his travels and celestial bearing, was not immune to the fad of ghetto couture. Trouble was, he didn't have any money, though he did have a sense of street economics and knew that drugs begat money, and money begat clothes, and all of this begat guns.

———◆·◆———

Give me that.

He snatched it from my palm.

Watch.

Thumb and forefinger in one easy motion. *Clack, click.* He handed the gun back to me. It weighed three times its diminutive size, impossibly dense: a semiautomatic black hole. I could not cock this three and a half inches of steel into potency. At that moment I wished for nothing more than to be back at home, a plate of slightly burned fish sticks and the remainder of the Guy de Maupassant (something about furniture flying around this poor sap's house) on my lap. But no—Stefan needed me for backup. On this *deal.* In *case.*

I wiped my palms on my jeans—probably just

sweaty is all, lemme get a good grip here . . . *Nothing*. I
can't rack the slide (that thing they do in the movies
where the hero holds the gun out, arms extended, or
next to his face and pulls back the thing on top, expos-
ing steel and a bit of the barrel); no strength in my grip,
my forearms, my will. I try again, knowing that this is
yet another test of physical strength for which my pathetic genes have left me ill equipped—I might as well
leap to the floor in a full handstand and crank out some
upside-down push-ups. I laugh timidly, deflecting, pretending that maybe I just don't have the mechanics
down—*it goes this way, right?* Grunting now, in full-out
effort, tongue jammed in the side of my mouth, I console myself with the assumption that Pepper from *Police
Woman* likely

    a) had the benefit of years of police acad-
       emy training

or,

    b) had used a revolver.

Stefan is fuming. We don't have time for this.
Now he flicks a lever on the top of the barrel, and a

fractional piece of it juts out at me—the ass end of a bullet secreted there, the words *.25 gr.apc.* stamped into its rear.

He flicks the lever back down.

Think you can handle that?

I nod yes, blithely, wondering what will happen if I have to shoot more than one person. I'm like Barney Fife with my lone bullet.

He eases shut his father's desk drawer, where from its underside, two minutes earlier, he had pulled the concealed Beretta.

Let's go.

Roye had guns hidden throughout the house: the .25 Beretta in the sitting room on the first floor, the .38 Special in a hallway closet on the second floor, and then there was a .357 Magnum, which I never did get to see, in a nightstand drawer somewhere, probably in his sanctum sanctorum on the third floor. Roye spent all of his time at home locked behind that door, watching Super TV and smoking enough marijuana to cure a wardful of glaucoma patients. Stefan, who had been briefed on handgun-safety precautions, was fastidious about double and triple checking chambers, magazines, and safeties. I never once felt at risk, until I started carrying.

Stefan had taken to wearing the requisite, gorgeous (if showy) three-quarter leather jackets, lambskin coats, and Nike Airs, which made him, and by extension me (we walked everywhere together), a moving target. He would never have even thought to avoid a given neighborhood, no matter its reputation—in fact, venturing into unknown dangerous ground gave him a nostril-flaring, shoulder-squaring jolt. He loved to test his own mettle, and by extension mine.

The sometimes gun in my pocket was a tacit acknowledgment that fists and reducible odds weren't all there ever would be; perforce, as portable life insurance for Stefan and me as we embarked on our new business. We were going to be singular stereotypes: poor, inner-city, black, Jewish, and European drug dealers.

Well, pot dealers. The Jewish kids at school enjoyed their smoke at rotating house parties, New Wave affairs redolent with insipid sensimilla and skinny ties, occasioned by parents who had jaunted off to the Caribbean or Boca. Stefan figured that some of his associations as ghetto bon vivant could supply him with cheap weed that once admixed with oregano, parsley flakes, or crabgrass could be sold for twice what we (he, but I was his best friend and shared the profits, if not the outlay) had paid for it.

Stefan did have a real job, carrying paraplegics around his neck the lengths of a pool every night, changing them back into their clothes, holding their dicks for them while they pissed, no matter the $15 dollar per hour pay rate. The plan was to take some of the money he had earned as a lifeguard and parlay that into a "lid" of marijuana (however much that was).

We left his house—I had the money and the Beretta—and sat for a few moments in the park next to the Murphy Homes, mapping out the plan for the evening: we would go to the housing projects where his "contact" was, pick up the marijuana, and then go to a house party being given by one of the A-course kids in Mt. Washington. There we would hit on some Jewesses, make some money, and leave, hopefully a little lighter in the scrotum and a little heavier in the wallet. I sat on the bench next to him while we dreamed our dreams and schemed our schemes, and watched as a man I knew from somewhere walked by. Stefan's words began to trail off, like a radio dialing through static, and the man hesitated as he passed. I recognized both the pause and the burnished ebony of his African features from my first day at The House, when he had turned and asked me *you wanna fight?* Later, from somewhere or someone, I had heard the name "Ricky" whispered in fearful tones. Ricky had clearly gotten a few years older, harder. As Stefan was still talking, oblivious, colors got brighter and the air took on a sibilant hiss; I still knew that pause, knew what it meant years before between two kids, but the world was different now and

FADE IN:

EXT. PARK BENCH--AFTERNOON

Ricky--long, lean, full of quiet menace--turns, retraces his steps back to the bench.

Stefan is talking--hasn't noticed him yet.

A shadow falls over the bench, long and sinister.

> RICKY
> Yeah. How much you got?

Stefan looks up. Leans back against the bench.

> STEFAN
> Brother, we're just talking here. Got nothing for you.

Ricky--expressionless--sighs. Unzips his windbreaker.

> RICKY
> Damn. You goin' make me take it from you?

Stefan--up now, moving away from the bench in a wide circle.

> STEFAN
> (to David)
> Go!

David moves behind the bench.

> RICKY
> You gonna have to stand still--a nigger ain't got all day.

Stefan--moving on the balls of his feet, keeping an arm's length between Ricky and himself.

                    STEFAN
                    (to David)
          David! Go! I'm not fucking
          around, move!

                    RICKY
          Why he got to go? He next.

                    DAVID
          No. I won't. I'm not.

Scared. But resolute. He jams his hand into his
pocket.

                    RICKY
                    Nigger hold still, let's do
                    this.

He swaggers in closer, leans into a loose box-
ing stance.

Stefan keeps his distance, his eyes flashing between Ricky, David, and that hand inside David's
jacket pocket.

                    STEFAN
                    (to David)
          I'm not gonna tell you again!

                    DAVID
          I'm not leaving!

A SMALL CROWD has gathered in front of the
housing project. Some point. Some laugh. Not a
Good Samaritan in the bunch.

Ricky stops.

                    RICKY
                    Why you don't stand still?
                    Hit me?

                    STEFAN
                    'Cause you a brother, that's
                    why.

Ricky laughs. A FEW PEOPLE on the sidelines
laugh along with him. Most ridiculous thing
they've ever heard.

> RICKY
> 'Cause I'm a . . . ?

Ricky looks at David.

> RICKY
> *He* ain't a brother.

He walks over. Slow. Deliberate. Like he's going to get the Sunday paper.

> STEFAN
> Run! Now!

David backs up, but he won't run. His hand is
outside of his pocket now, his palm full of the
tiny Beretta.

> RICKY
> What you got?

David's eyes go wide, he raises his arm--

> STEFAN
> Hey, *nigga.*

Ricky turns.

> RICKY
> *That's* what I'm talking
> about.

They square off, inches from each other, Stefan's hands loose and dangling at his side,
now--

> MAN'S VOICE (O.S.)
> Youngbloods!

A HOUSING MAINTENANCE WORKER, fifties, black,
storms over.

Ricky backs off, an ivory grin across his face,
and bops the other way through the park.

                    MAINTENANCE WORKER
          Don't fuck with him.

                    STEFAN
          We weren't.

David comes over--hands empty--ashen.

                    MAINTENANCE WORKER
          He from over Murphy Homes,
          nigga need to stay there.

                    DAVID
          He lives at the Murphy Homes?

Stefan watches Ricky's figure disappear down
the alley.

                                        CUT TO:

INT. MEMORIAL APARTMENTS ELEVATOR--MOMENTS
LATER

David and Stefan watch the floors click off on
the lighted display.

TWO,

                    DAVID
          It's crazy, is what it
          is . . .

THREE,

                    DAVID
          You know how many people I
          heard got shot there last
          year?

FOUR . . .

DING! As the elevator doors open.

INT. HALLWAY--MOVING WITH THEM--SAME TIME

> STEFAN
> No . . . how many?

> DAVID
> Lots. I say we forget the whole--

> STEFAN
> --Jesus--you douche today?

They get to the end of the hallway, ring the bell on door number 413.

David removes the Beretta and an envelope of money from his jacket pocket.

> DAVID
> Here. Why do I have to carry money, and the gun?

> STEFAN
> You been by a mirror lately? It's called "going against type."

The door opens, and MAE, a tiny woman in her eighties, waits for her hug.

> STEFAN
> (sotto voce)
> Might wanna put those away.
> (to Mae)
> Hi Grandma!

David fumbles the packages, barely manages to get them stuffed back into his pocket before Mae and Stefan shut the door in his face.

> CUT TO:

INT. MAE'S APARTMENT--MOMENTS LATER

David paces in the living room, while Mae sits in a

recliner in front of the TV, twiddling her thumbs.

A FAIR-HAIRED BOY OF TEN sits Indian-style on
the floor watching TV. This is KHARI.

Stefan comes out of the bedroom, pocketing an
address book.

> DAVID
>
> And?

> STEFAN
>
> It's on.

> DAVID
>
> You're really gonna make
> us--?

> MAE
>
> --You boys going out? It's
> supposed to be chilly.

> STEFAN
>
> Yes, ma'am. I'm taking David
> to a party.

> MAE
>
> Where?

> STEFAN
>
> With some kids from school,
> in Mt. Washington.

> MAE
>
> Oh, pardon me! I'm just one
> of the hoi polloi.

They all laugh, except for David.

> DAVID
> (sotto voce)
> Why don't you tell her where
> you're taking me first . . .

                    KHARI
Where you guys going? Can I
come?

                    MAE
What's that?

                    STEFAN
Oh, he's just nervous. Wants
to make a good impression.

                    MAE
Maybe he needs some makeup.

More chuckles.

                    MAE
You know what my mother used
to tell me before I went out?

                    DAVID
                    (wearily)
Yes.

                    STEFAN
No. What?

                    MAE
                    (as Mae speaks, David
                    lip-synchs along)
"A little bit of powder, a
little bit of paint, makes
you look like what you
ain't."

                    STEFAN
You never needed a bit of
makeup.

                    MAE
Oh, who are you fooling, I
look like the wreck of the
Hesperus.

                         STEFAN
                      (with a nod)
          Well . . . adventures await.

David follows him sullenly to the door.

                         DAVID
             Dreamy.

                         KHARI
             Can I come?

                         STEFAN
                      (to Mae as he shuts
                      the door)
             Bye Grandma . . .
                      (to Khari)
             Do some push-ups or some-
             thing.

                                        CUT TO:

EXT. THE MURPHY HOMES--NIGHT

A garrison-like cluster of public housing towers. There is chain-link fencing along the entire facade, covering windows, balconies, every
way in or out. The state pen is more inviting.

Stefan and David stand outside the entrance to
one of the towers.

David attempts a disaffected posture of street
cool, but looks more like he has Bell's palsy.

                         STEFAN
             You wanna wait, or come with?

David starts to answer, but sees, slinking
through the courtyard, what looks like the SIL-
HOUETTE of Ricky.

                         DAVID
             That second thing.

                                        CUT TO:

EXT. MURPHY HOMES HALLWAY--EVENING

A BLACK MAN in his forties gives Stefan a
black-power salute.

                    STEFAN
          Thanks, brother.

Stefan pockets a baggie half-filled with marijuana.

                    MAN
          No doubt.
                    (vis-à-vis David)
          You might not wanna bring him
          around here no more.

He shuts the door.

Stefan puts his arm around David's shoulder and
walks away.

                    STEFAN
          That wasn't as bad as all
          that, was it?

David forces a weak smile.

                                        CUT TO:

INT. POSH HOUSE--NIGHT

Fifty or so TEENAGE KIDS, mostly white, spill
through the well-appointed house.

MUSIC (The Jam, Prince, Nena, The English Beat)
BLARES from a record player, and pockets of
kids in various stages of making out sprinkle
the living room, den, kitchen.

David wanders through, sipping at an empty Coke
can just to have something to do.

He talks to no one, no one talks to him, until,

                         GIRL'S VOICE (O.S.)
               Hey--David!

A girl, all tits and ass, grabs him by the elbow.

                         DAVID
               He's through that door.

                         GIRL
               Thanks!

And she is gone like she was never there.

Over the music, THE SOUND OF SHOUTING and MEN'S
VOICES.

A stampede of KIDS, scattering in every direction.

An irate GIRL of fifteen is at the front door,
her shoulder hard against it.

The door is open about six inches, and a flashlight beam plays into the room through the gap.

                         GIRL
               I KNOW MY RIGHTS! My father
               is a--

                         COP
               Then you know we have the
               right to break this door down
               if we feel--

Beyond the open door--the glint of silver
badges and the swirl of squad car lights.

David snatches his coat from a couch and races
through the kitchen and out the

EXT. POSH HOUSE-BACKYARD--SAME TIME

Kids running in every direction--flashlight
beams ricochet off the dense thicket of trees,
illuminating the blur of legs and arms.

David looks around wildly--doesn't know where to go.

He feels in his pocket. Shit. The gun. The pot.

He takes out the gun and the baggy--goes to dump it behind some bushes--

                    COP
          Hey!

A flashlight beam hits him square in the face.

                    MALE VOICE (O.S.)
          Yo!

The COP turns, his light landing on STEFAN--who jumps up in the air and clicks his heels together. He takes off.

The COP whirls his light back into the thicket and sees

Nothing.

                              CUT TO:

INT. CITY BUS--LATER

Stefan and David, alone on a deserted transit bus. The suburbs roll quietly by.

                    STEFAN
          And *you* thought this was a
          bad idea.

David stares at him. Stony. Silent. And then both boys

Crack the fuck up.

The BUS DRIVER glances in his rearview at his lone hysterical passengers. Shakes his head.

                              FADE OUT.

CHAPTER XII

DEARLY BELOVED

Quitting came easily to me. While my father, grandmother, friends, and guidance counselor assured me that dropping out of high school would prove my ruination, getting my GED seemed a more reasonable option than watching everyone I knew graduate without me. My years of truancy and negligent study habits caught up with me eventually, and I was left back. I wasn't particularly popular—my abasement would hardly have been a *scandale*—but I needed to be in control, even in my disintegration. I stayed for the first few months of City's fall 1984 year—my eleventh-grade redux—before leaving for the shadowy pastures of the ebony league. Turns out, I would go to college after all, though in a manner that surprised even me.

In order to receive a GED (Stefan referred to this document as a "Good Enough Diploma"), the errant scholar must be absent from his previous learning facility for at least ninety days. No problem. When I left City, it was winter, and not being of the age or inclination to secure employment, I spent the remainder of those months reading—boning up for the test (I was certain that the complete works of Joseph Wambaugh and Saul Bellow would prove germane to my success)—and masturbating. My father had always contended that boredom was *the inability to deal with one's surroundings*, so I made every attempt at industry.

While accompanying my grandmother to the physician one day, I was left alone in an empty surgery off to one side. I crept into the room, rifled through the drawers, and found a cache of latex surgical gloves that immediately presented themselves as objects with no little variety of uses. I jammed a fistful into my pants and returned to the waiting room, chuckling lasciviously as I flipped through a hard-used *Redbook* magazine.

Except for my stay at my grandmother's, I had had the same foam bed, the lower portion of the bunk I had shared with Elijah, since I was four years old. Now relocated to my third-floor bedroom at The House, my feet dangled from its end, the sliver of two-inch foam between me and the wooden slats separating the discs in my back and abrading my bones while I read/slept. Rigidity being the mother of invention, as I tossed fitfully one night it occurred to me that my desire for someone (or *something*, as it were; I could not afford to be picky) soft and squishy was just below me. I remembered the booty of surgical gloves. Struck by divinely prurient inspiration, and knowing the basic properties of foam and its recoverability, I slashed a slit of a few inches in length in the middle of the foam, in between two of the slats, and then filled a surgical glove with Vaseline petroleum jelly, which I inserted into the slit, fingers first. The opening, a primed, latex labia spread wide and beckoning on the surface of the mattress, was where, in a feral wave of toe-curling thrusts, I had my first bucking orgasm by dint of an outside agent. *No glove, no love.**

So were spent the ninety days and nights I waited for the test. On a spring day, I, along with thirty or forty parolees, unwed mothers, and mouth-breathers, took my GED examination. The questions being of this ilk:

The First President of the United States of America was:

    A) George Washington

    B) Grover Washington, Jr.

    C) George Jefferson

I passed quite easily and was soon the proud recipient of a piece of paper.

Through his travels (for he was a "people" person) Stefan had become acquainted with an administrator at Baltimore's Coppin State College, a barely accredited all-black community college in such academic disrepute that my father referred to it as the *high school on the hill.*

The tuition for a semester at Coppin was six hundred

---

*It was unglamorous, and wholly pathetic, but I have, in the years hence, which have obviated (somewhat) the need for such lurid contrivances, had much, much worse.

dollars. A down payment of two hundred dollars was required to secure admittance, an amount equivalent to two thousand million dollars to me and my family. My benefactor and Stefan's friend, Mr. B——, who turned out to be a closeted, mincing homosexual, graciously wrote me a check. Deeply gratified, I was also deeply concerned. Mercenary enough to realize that I would do *nearly* anything to guarantee some small bit of insurance against becoming a vocational school graduate, or manqué stand-up comedian, I would not allow my sphincter to be vitiated as a result of money offered. I nevertheless took the money, and my misgivings, and registered for classes.

For a moment, I forgot that I was the lightest-hued person, with the exception of some of the white teachers. The school was nearly 100 percent black, the only exception among the student body a willowy, pockmarked white girl, who hurried about the campus like a specter. On registration day, we all gathered in an empty conference hall, where the different classes on offer were represented by single desks to which a piece of paper with the course name and number had been affixed. Behind each desk was the instructor for the course, who answered questions and personally added pupils' names to their rosters. I asked the smartly appointed black woman professor at the "Introduction to American Literature" table about her reading list and, realizing that I had already read most of the selections, promptly signed up. By the end of registration day, I had a basic math class and three varieties of literature on my schedule. My plan for math, my mortal enemy, mirrored the stratagem with which I had plotted my entire stay at Coppin State College: I would use the lax institution to fulfill basic college "core" courses before transferring somewhere whiter, better (I saw no distinction between those adjectives). I hoped that the regimen at Coppin would be insipid enough for me to eke out a passing grade, and thus forgo the ravages of math at my future institution (I had champagne visions of NYU, Haverford, or Swarthmore on a beer drinker's budget).

I did very well at Coppin, passing for the first time in a very long time, if also not *passing*. The campus was composed of so many shades of black, brown, ochre, and yellow that there I was just another brother. No way could I pass. For the semester I was there, and without any real choice, I allowed myself to be black. Whereas whites had asked me what I was in order to find a reason to exclude me, blacks looked at even the lightest high-yellow octoroon as another potential soldier should the revolution one day come. Had I tried to deny it, the students at Coppin would have seen through my *boojie* attempt at passing and torn me limb from limb.

It was both liberating and frustrating to discover that I was blacker than I had ever realized. The cultural influences of my father, grandmother, my entire home life, had leached into my consciousness, unbidden. I felt at home, and yet not at home, as though I were a funambulist, ill equipped to trod solid ground. Coppin showed up how inexpert I was at communicating with my own people: in primary and secondary school, I had only observed my black friends from the distance of my adopted white skin and culture, afraid that my active participation in their world would taint me, like the threat that having pulled a face it would stay that way. At Coppin, I was afraid of dialectical gaffes, or, more probably, coming off as less than cool. My father's prophecies were becoming Delphic in their precision. He had told me to make friends with *all different kinds of people*, and I had scoffed. Now, sitting among my fellow students, who were funny, and shrewd, and a hundred times more motivated than I was, I was at a loss for words.

My favorite teacher, Sam Jones, a lachrymose older white man with silvery hair, a bushy mustache, and a voice like whiskey-filtered Lucky Strikes, took the same bus home with me every day and razzed me incessantly about my youthful appearance. As my birthday neared, he said he'd take me out for a beer. I reminded him that the drinking age was eighteen, and he rasped with a wink, *Not where I go.* On that breezy November evening he met me, as promised, at a tenebrous hole called The Drinkery, and bought me a pint of lager, my first. I wobbled home after that single beer, feeling like a real dyed-in-the-wool bohemian intellectual.

After my demoralizing stint at City, where everyone seemed to know more than I did, I relished my role at

Coppin as the "smart guy." The teachers and I carried on lengthy discussions in the middle of class, and even though I felt (justifiably) resentful eyes piercing the back of my head, and the color rushing to my face, I could not stop. The same smartly appointed "American Literature" professor asked the class one day about their favorite cult films and was greeted by a dinning silence. I raised my hand to offer up *Putney Swope*, and from there the professor and I, like old soldiers who hadn't seen each other since boot camp, tossed around *Sweet Sweetback's Badasssss Song*, the genius of Godfrey Cambridge (my father had known him, and of course I managed to artlessly slip this in), the film *Three the Hard Way*, and the inerrant photographic eye of Gordon Parks.

A genial young man, after one such exchange, leaned over, and not unkindly asked, Three the Hard Way . . . *that playing out at the suburbs or something*? The boy and I spoke for a few moments, and I was both inexplicably touched and not a little ashamed when I saw that he had entered, in an earnest hand, the names of some of the people and things I had mentioned into his notebook. And then it hit me. All at once I was that which I hated and that which I had wanted to become: I was now the insufferably voluble Jew at the head of the class.* Jesus. Oy.

Like the beautiful girl who stares into a mirror and

---

*I use the word *Jew* because my initiation into the world of academic enfants terribles was colored thus; and because, warring id and all, I am a Jew, by their laws if not their culture.

sees her willowy limbs laden with blubber, I saw my display of smarts as the disavowal of what it meant to be young, black, and male. I then fell victim to the same intellectual anorexia that has starved the black urban male for generations. I began to equate intelligence (here I must refrain at all cost from imprecision—in my case, I had begun to equate and disdain the *display* of intellect, *not* the possession of said) with uncool, which is the definition of white. I found myself theatrically scratching my head in puzzlement at instructors' softball questions, or else mumbling my answers in a halting, self-disparaging manner, as though admitting that only by freak happenstance did I come to be in possession of such esoterica. My cultural vision was becoming blurred and perspicacious all at once. I read, wrote, and figured out all by myself what exactly the "problem" part of the "Negro problem" was. Black people don't read.*

As the 1980s lumbered to its midpoint, the scions of the *Baltimore Afro-American* empire decided to change the tenor of the paper, watering it down with so much bug-eyed striving and refulgent civic pride that my father could brook his job as managing editor no further. Baltimore had at one time a great population of black entrepreneurs, artists, and tradesmen who were now but a hoary list of names and deeds trotted out—usually in

---

*Lurid, caramel tales of assignation and incarceration, or books sold from card tables outside subway stations, do not count.

February—as proof that all was not lost; in fact, most of it was, and hopelessly. The new *Afro-American*'s "fluff" pieces on this or that councilman or "Afro-clean-block" winner were not advancing *the cause*. Still wanting to peel back the rotted layers of onionskin that segregated the city, my father struck out on his own, founding, along with his then girlfriend Kimberly T——, the biweekly paper *Baltimore City Fare*. Get it?

I did not care for Ms. T, a keen young reporter (at twenty-eight exactly half my father's age) he had poached from the *Afro*; though she was kind, generous, and funny, she was also indisputably black: Kenyan features, short lustrous Afro—to my hateful eyes, a pickaninny. Despite whatever "black like you" succor I stole from my classmates at Coppin, I was as infected by my racism as ever, having treated only the symptoms, not the disease.

Historically (as far back as my knowledge of him extended, all of seventeen years), I had only seen my father with white women. Until the point he met Kimberly, my father had, in my opinion, exercised prudent choices in only that area of his life. To someone as fatuously deranged as myself, this made him just a little bit less "black," and, well, every little bit helped. Kimberly sent me into a violent spiral; I became the verso of the unnamed narrator of Ellison's *Invisible Man*, maniacally swirling the paint that provided my cover until the offending dot was absorbed, obliterated, etiolated, expiated.

My daily life with the two of them and Khari, who was now entering preadolescence, affirmed my "blackness," and made me want to separate the skin from my body. I feared the (somewhat correct) assumption by the outside world that we were just a variegated black family on our way to the Rustler Steakhouse. Packed among them, there could be no wiggle room for Arab fathers and Jewish mothers, no hopes that the world would judge me based not on the content of my character but on the color of my skin, which, depending upon its closest neighbor, was either white by inference or black by implication.

Convinced that there was a black literati in urban Baltimore clamoring for a smart, alternative voice to the *Afro*, my father formed a corporation with the ennobling moniker Indigo Publications. He and Kimberly inveigled, wheedled, and cajoled friends, and friends of friends, into purchasing advertising space in *City Fare*. Just as I had deluded myself, for about thirteen seconds, into thinking that The House had been a practicable endeavor, so did I, for roughly the same length of time, get swept up in this folly. I helped my father and Kimberly deliver copies of *City Fare* to the myriad black businesses they had guilted into subsidization, only to see the newsprint yellow, unread, beneath the lurid glare of the same storefront windows. I spent late nights with my father at Howard Johnson cafés, dreaming up how best to market the paper. These late-night trips when he treated me to blue-plate specials were my favorite times with my pop. How could this man—the people he had known, the things he had seen—be reduced to this Podunk town, food stamps, and the occasional "splurge" on clam strips and sundaes? Something, somewhere, was not right.

He talked about writing on the new "nonmusic"—rap—which was fast becoming the soundtrack to urban life. Though he loathed it, he believed it would be a good way to reach a disaffected readership. I knew that his strategy—*Hey gang! Let's put out a paper!*—was perforce doomed, little more than a Busby Berkeley approach to publishing.

Inner-city black folks were not interested in *City Fare*, just as they were barely interested in the *Afro*, which limped along by dint of history and precedent. Thus *City Fare* died a quiet, ignominious death, plunging my father and our family—already on welfare since my father's departure from the *Afro*—into indigence. My father felt no shame at our joining the welfare rolls; in fact, there was an almost smug sense of entitlement about it, a snarling, *fuck 'em, the least they can do for me after four hundred years of this shit*. I did not share his hauteur. The way I saw it, he, an able-bodied (qualifiedly, but you get my point), mercurially intelligent, and experienced man, chose a risky speculative venture that did not warrant government subsidy. I honestly don't know, however, which of us was right.

Meanwhile my grandmother's apartment began to take on the frayed disrepair of a flophouse. Always a fastidious woman who wore smart polyester dresses and had her hair done once a week in the Memorial Gardens beauty parlor, she was now rail thin, fairly haunting her tattered housecoats, her hair stringy and limp around her neck. Her mind, which had been as clear as a mostly sunny day, was now clouded over. She would shake her head in her chair, snapping her fingers and tapping her noggin in the hope that the ghost names, places, dates could be reanimated by sheer will. One day I knocked on the door to her apartment, and she shuffled to it, opened it, stared me full in the face for several seconds, and hissed, *Who are you?* before turning away without waiting for an answer. I sat in the stairwell for a few moments after that, grinding my fingernails into bloody half-moons in my palms.

Stefan graduated in June of '85 (as I should have), but before leaving the country, he and I applied for jobs at a nascent hotel, still under construction, along Baltimore's (also nascent) inner harbor. Stefan applied as a lifeguard, and I, with "references" from exotic Gallic cafés and bistros, applied as a room-service waiter. By the time the Sheraton Inner Harbor Hotel hired me that July for my first job, Stefan was long gone. There I made money, or what was to me money—in the vicinity of $60 to $100 a day in tips—for the first time in my life. I worked twelve-hour shifts, from dinner, to late night, to breakfast service, which I would follow with a full round of classes. I caught naps on the restaurant's banquettes, or in a heap on my grandmother's couch. I now stayed at The House only as a last resort, the (to my eyes) sham family of my father, Kimberly, and Khari in that hovel far beyond the powers of my understanding.

I had paid my second-semester tuition at Coppin with a shoe box full of crumpled ones and fives. The registrar was not amused. My benefactor from the prior semester found me in class one day and beckoned me outside. The Damoclean cock—I mean sword—which had hung over my ass and head was about to fall. He took me to his office and asked me how my classes were going, and *if I had forgotten all about him.* I laughed and said, *No, just busy is all.*

He swiveled in his chair and said, in a dreamy, faraway drawl, *What do you think we oughta do about that loan I gave you?*

I fidgeted for a minute and felt a bulge in my pocket. I reached in and pulled out my tips from the past three days. *Pay it*, I shrugged. For once I had the right rejoinder, at the right time.

———◆———

This was the mid-eighties, when the light-skinned El Debarge look was in vogue, so I rationalized that while I did my time at Coppin, I could at least—and at long last—get some pussy. At the tender age of seventeen, I had the requisite curls ("good hair"), green eyes, and buttery complexion, but otherwise looked hopelessly puerile. Some of the girls may have wanted to pinch my cheeks or smile wistfully at me, but none were willing to help flush the old vas deferens. I can't really blame them. Fey and wan, especially in the black community, are hardly erotic stimulants.

I lacquered my hair with parching mousses and unctuous gels to form a riot of curls atop my skull, and pouted and sulked my way through the corridors, hoping that my smoldering yet demurring glances would inflame scores of young Lisa Bonet/Vanessa Williams/Jennifer Beals–types into my spindly arms. It is a testament to the incalculable effect Prince and the movie *Purple Rain* had on my sexual self-consciousness (here was someone able to defy the very Stefan-like conventions of male attractiveness, i.e., masculine-protector, which had kept me from women these last few years) that I actually thought this ethereal androgyne approach could work. Somewhere in my unchecked ego, I had forgotten to account for the fact that Prince was *a fucking genius* rock star, which may have accounted for the scores of vertical smiles that glistened before him. Now that I was ready to embrace (does a leporine fuck count as an embrace?) my sisters—or the light-skinned ones, at any rate—they wanted nothing to do with me.

———•———

By the end of my final semester at Coppin, I had all A's and B's. The week of my finals, I was asleep in the student union, curled up on a couch, half listening to the conversations going on around me. Two girls were gossiping on the sofa next to me. One of them whispered urgently, *Did you hear about that teacher? The one that got killed?*

I sat bolt upright, interrupting them. I didn't need to loiter long enough to hear the end of their story, because somehow I already knew. When I arrived at Mr. Jones's Comparative Lit class and the smart black lady who had taught American Literature the previous semester was behind his desk, a pained expression on her face, I considered it just notification of not-so-next of kin.

Mr. Jones had spent a night of hard drinking at The Drinkery, I would later read in the papers (a friend's death practically the only event that could inspire such an action), and had invited a young man back to his apartment. After they had sex, the man bound him, fastened a ligature around his neck, and squeezed the life out of him. Before I read that, all I knew was that my favorite teacher had been murdered, and that I had gotten close to him, which I tried not to do very often. I remembered that the day before he was murdered, while we waited in the freezing wind for the bus, stamping our feet, the remnants of a cold I'd had caused me to cough up great globs of phlegm.

He winced at my hacking, and I said, *Ugh, I think some faggot spit in my coffee and gave me AIDS.* I suppose I had thought this was blithe, or coarsely humorous. It was 1986, and all anyone knew from AIDS was Liberace and Rock Hudson. I didn't know Sam was gay. I was an asshole. *Jesus Christ, you're an asshole* were, in fact, the final words he ever spoke to me.

———•———

With the mountain of tips I had accrued from working room service, I moved out of my grandmother's and The House and in with an achingly beautiful cocktail waitress from the hotel's garish nightclub, Impulse (if that is any indication of the pleasures found before its bank of video screens and upon its strobed dance floor). She (maddeningly) viewed me as nothing more than half the rent, while I viewed her as an unattainable real woman (she was twenty-five), manumission from the life I had known, and masturbatory fuel. I had nothing but a sack of clothes and a few books, which I moved all of three blocks (a universe) back into a brownstone walk-up on Bolton Hill's Park Avenue. I was home.

The day I left, my grandmother was practically immobile, very nearly at the end of her ability to live among the self-sufficient. She had had a series of small strokes, a few of which I had witnessed, and which themselves had almost terrified me toward flight. My grandmother Mae, her face frozen in my memory and above my desk as I write these words, a color photograph alive with that crooked smile and eyes as mirthful and dancing as any Irish drunk's, had begun to forget my name, sometimes answering my rung doorbell and asking, *What do you want from me?* Other times, during the worst of these episodes, when her left or right arm would palsy and flop helplessly against her side, her eyes lolling back into her skull, I would stay, and whisper, *Gramma? Gramma?* until the tremors stopped and she floated back from her Stygian depths to a diminished version of the life she had known. I knew one of these would be her last, and I knew I could not be there to witness it. As I packed my meager belongings, she held out her hand at the bedside and I took it. *You—you're the one,* she smiled, as though to tell me that whether I knew it or not, *she* did, and she wasn't going to let me forget it. That was the last time I saw her.

CHAPTER XIII

ACE IN THE HOLE

Don't come in my mouth, Heather says.

I nod dumbly, words beyond me, which I guess passes for agreement because she retraces her mouth back to me, swallowing me to the pubis.

Ten . . . nine . . . eight . . .

On the TV next to her bed, Dick Clark is counting down another *New Year's Rockin' Eve.* The white light–encrusted orb is making its plodding descent down the pole in Times Square. Heather's hand tightens around me, her fist swirling circles as her mouth glides down to meet it before retreating.

Six . . . five . . .

When I asked her what she was getting me for Christmas, she'd said I had to wait for New Year's Eve.

Four . . . three . . .

Heather! Open the fuckin' door!

It's her brother Marc, whom I've never met, slapping the door with his palm.

She wipes her mouth with the back of her hand, pushes herself away, and goes to the door, a final glance at me to make sure I've put myself away. In my haste,

I've lashed my cock upright against my belly, my belt cinched around it like a rodeo lasso.

She opens the door partway; he pushes the rest.

The ball drops. It's 1987. People on TV are going screaming yellow zonkers. I can hear male voices downstairs cheering. Off in the suburban air, there is the crack of gunshots and the sound of faint huzzahs.

On the edge of the bed, feigning a keen interest in the televised activities four hundred miles away in New York City, I can feel the semen grudgingly recede back to wherever it comes from, like a river of magma forced back up a volcano. Marc holds out two bottles of Moosehead beer, his fingertips stuck in their mouths.

Happy New Year, right? he smiles, all menace and cheer. He's nineteen. *Big*. Feathered baby shit–brown hair and a Dokken T-shirt, acid-washed blue jeans the color of his eyes.

Heather takes the beers, hands me one.

He raises his bottle, studying me intently over the lip as he toasts.

I cup my thumb and forefinger around the lip of the bottle, trying to minimize the contact between Marc's fingers (God only knows where they've been) and my lips. I take a swig. Half of it dribbles down my shirt.

Where you from?

———◆———

Heather was a bantam nymphet, with fat rings of auburn hair and shoulders as smooth as loomed silk, one of which she kept perennially bared in the *Flash-dance* style, a torturous reminder that everything that mattered—all the prime cuts, so to speak—were still out of sight, just out of reach. She had transferred to City two years earlier (I had already dropped out) and almost immediately became a prurient cause célèbre. Like all girls who were sure of their sexuality, she had made it her first order of duty, her orientation, if you will, to fuck Stefan exactly one day after her arrival.

Heather landed like a flower in that desert and was soon desired by all, if had only by Stefan, and only for about three weeks. After Stefan graduated and left for Europe, I could not shake my status as gooseberry. I remained a perfectly trued third wheel, rendered impotent even by his ghost. Heather and I would go to the movies, congregate at the inner harbor (which had matured into a full-blown irritant along Baltimore's downtown waterfront), chat on the phone—basically whatever it was eunuchs and courtesans did to kill time. Oddly, though Heather had known Stefan was black, she seemed unaware of *what I was*. Poor kid—she had a right to her opinion, and besides, who was she going to believe, me or her lying eyes?

I did little (actually, nothing) to disabuse her of her assumptions, so when she bitched and moaned about how Stefan had treated her so shabbily, and didn't he know what her father, no, forget that, her brothers would do if they ever found out she was *fuckin' a nigger?* I nodded in solemn accordance. Beauty has a way of making even a woman's most repugnant qualities endearing, thus I endured her execrable laments, hoping the "shoulder to cry on" approach would eventually lead to a tentative meeting of inflamed lips; which might segue to a swollen nipple placed between my parted teeth; which might lead, penultimately, to a grazing, fervent inhalation of labia and extract of vulva, capped off by urgent (though tender) rutting.

This was the plan, yet so far my endless patience had yielded little except the considerable boost to my ego that having arm candy of that quality afforded me. I had begun to form a stratagem around this time in regard to women: Contextual Seduction. If I positioned myself as a harmless male acquaintance, while observing strict gender roles, I could confuse the poor seraphs' biological hardware, supplanting their notion of hapless buddy into chivalric leading man. Doors were gallantly thrust open, even if it meant tripping over the girl herself in order to get there in time, bus seats were proffered (cars were not to be in my life until my twenties), orders on her behalf imperiously recited to justifiably horrified waiters, all while the collegial veneer of platonic friendship sparkled. In all things, I was trying to convey a subliminal hint: *You, young lady, are letting some perfectly good dick go to waste.* I rationalized that if they had only wanted me for who I was (like I knew), I would never have had to resort to being such a creep.

My guile did teach me one thing: girls loved nothing more than to be confused, as good an emotional state as any to be mistaken for attraction. To my eventual heart-break, the two emotions were often spent in close combat with each other until the smoke cleared, leaving my intended with an embarrassing *froideur* toward me.* If a man could master the confluence of confusion and attraction, parlaying it into a lasting emotional state, average-looking nonmillionaires could one day have a shot at coupling.

Despite a handful of near misses, I had never been in the presence of a naked woman, or been naked in the presence of *anyone*, save the fig leaf–inducing shame of Stefan et al. in high school/dojo locker rooms. As I have noted before, my body had proved dilatory in the dispensation of secondary sexual characteristics, so I had, in my early to mid-teens, resorted to a pitiful bit of legerdemain in order to convince others that I was a "man."

My grandmother had a collection of filamentary black hairnets, which, if bunched up, took on the texture of coarse human hair. On the mornings when I knew there to be some activity that would require my full dishabille, I affixed two or three of her hairnets to my pubis via a Magic Marker–blackened rubber band, and would wear the itchy, choking contraption for the entire

---

*Once, one of these girls I'd "confused" into loving me actually snapped out of it in my presence, as though given a safety word by a hypnotist stationed under the bed.

day. Of course, depending on the zeal, or degree of attention with which I had applied my merkin *pour l'homme*, I either wound up with a wandering, mangy bush, which lent my joint the appearance of having gone through an enervating round of chemotherapy, or a furry cock-ring. Erections begun in the latter state were immune even to thoughts of dead babies or naked grandmothers, and were perforce only diminished by a gimping rush to the boys' bathroom and the freeing of my member.

Eventually, I developed everything in its proper place, and lacked only for company. With Heather, I had been steadfastly chumming the waters for weeks, waiting for a bite. That Christmas I gave her a turquoise bracelet, which cost all of seven dollars, though I suppose she found the gesture sweet, if somewhat awkward. Unaware that we were on gift-giving terms, she had simply winked and said that she'd give me my present on New Year's Eve.

———◆———

Exasperated, Heather answers her brother: *Marc, I told you, he goes to my school.*

Marc sucks foam expertly from the top of his beer. This family, it would seem, is not without its talents. *That don't tell me where he's from.*

Bolton Hill, I answer, now far from hard.

That near downtown?

Sort of.

He turns his attention to Dick celebrating with

Daryl Hall. Without even looking at me: *Make a beer run with us.*

It doesn't sound like a question.

Marc, it's New Year's Eve, Heather says, her voice catching.

Three other boys crowd the doorway behind him now. I recognize two of them as Heather's other brothers; one of them is Tim, the other one I haven't yet met. They range in age from maybe sixteen to twenty-two, all metal-heads like Marc (I spot a long-sleeved Ronny James Dio T-shirt and a jean jacket with a Scorpions patch embroidered on its sleeve), and they're all very drunk.

This him? one of them slobbers through thick lips and heavy lids.

Marc waves me out. *Let's go,* he says, *don't forget who gave you that beer you're drinking.*

Marc, Heather starts, a question or a plea mingling with his name.

I wonder why we take two cars to get the beer. I'm with Marc in the front seat of his Tercel. His brothers and their friend follow behind. We're going about seventy miles an hour down a two-lane stretch of strip mall–flanked road, passing many places advertising beer; we stop at none of them. Marc takes a hard left onto a smaller road, fishtailing into the oncoming lane before righting us. I grab the handle above the door as casually as I can, like a professional race car passenger. *Watch this,* Marc says, shifting into fifth as we near a crest. Now we're airborne, an anvil dropped into my lower intestine, my palm against the ceiling to keep my head from making contact. We land in a shower of sparks and I hear the car behind us take the same flight, hoots and hollers and the *ka-chunk* of shock absorbers.

We pull into a macadam lot under a graffiti-strewn bridge, the two cars facing each other like a Detroit bull and Japanese matador. We all pile out, Marc clambering onto a rock where he stands, pissing a huge arcing stream of processed Moosehead beer into the black. I realize we're over a river or a creek or something, the car's head-lights catching just the close shore of the water.

It's colder than Eskimo pussy out here, Tim says, blow-ing on his fingers and popping the trunk of his Corolla. The other two stamp their feet against the cold and walk toward the edge of the road we came in on.

So where're you from again? Marc asks, zipping him-self up.

Bolton Hill. It's near—

Yeah, you said that. I hear the trunk slam shut be-hind me. To my left, Heather's other brother and his friend have fanned out on either side of the roadway. They watch for cars, smoking Marlboro Reds and whis-pering.

What are you? Marc asks.

What do you mean? I'm stalling now.

Tim leans against his car, the far side, so that I can't see his hands. I wonder what, if anything, he pulled from that trunk. I hear three Morse code–like dings, Tim's car stereo splitting the air with Rush launching into "YYZ," a hard-rock Wagnerian *Ring* cycle. I see Tim pull his hand away from the volume knob. For some reason, out here in the wooded darkness, they want it loud.

Marc comes closer. *What are you?*—trying to keep it light, like the answer doesn't matter, a mere formality.

The music crashes into the brittle air. I've been here before; I know there's a right answer, a wrong answer, and an answer that's not quite right, but not as bad as being wrong.

I remember my father's words to me, his augury that day in the park, that as my features became more "African," I will no longer *be able to travel freely through that little world of mine.* Maybe this was that day, I thought, eliminating as a possibility my first answer and with it any assertion of straight-up whiteness: the olive of my skin and the swell of my lips won't stand up to a claim of *Mayflower* descendancy. The second answer—that I'm mixed, half black and half—well, no need to worry about trying to explain away the other half, because as soon as the word *black* issues from my lips, the mystery of whatever it is Tim pulled from his trunk will be balefully solved.

I go with answer number three: *Jesus Christ, don't tell me you care that I'm half Jewish.* I land hard on the word *Jewish*, bait-and-switching them with their lesser prejudice; if black is melanoma, then Jewish is a mole.

Marc stops and looks over my shoulder to Tim.

Tim, from behind me, *What's the other half?*

I shift my weight uncomfortably, a wracking, full-blown case of blue-balls setting in.

Episcopalian.

They share a stare, and when their blue eyes meet mine, they're as hard and pointed as bullets through my skull.

The woofers in the back of Tim's car are pushing the leaden air around us, the cold stabbing every amplified note past my inner ear and into my brain. If they are going to do this, come at me with flesh and bone and whatever is in Tim's hand, I wish they'd do it now, while I can still feel my fists and make some last accounting of myself. I sell them what they want to hear, one last time. *Dude, I like Rush and all, but it's fuckin' cold out here.* Dropping my g's, faking a bit of the accent I've heard bouffanted waitresses and tattooed mechanics use throughout Baltimore.

Marc laughs. *You're a Heeb?* He's relieved. I laugh a little myself.

Only on my mother's side, and I never met the bitch. Now I'm drumming a bit of Neal Peart's solo on the car's hood, partly from nerves, partly to keep enough feeling in my hands in case I have to come out swinging.

Marc laughs again. He nods at Tim, who goes back to the trunk of his car. I never see what he puts back, just as I never saw what he took out.

Marc wags a finger at me jovially. *I knew it.*

He pulls out his car keys. I hear Tim's trunk slam behind me. Marc stops and points again. *Favorite song?*

"The Spirit of Radio," I answer.

Tim comes around, his car keys in his hand. *Yeah, but nothing beats this solo.* And now he drums some of the patterns on the roof of his car. He's crappy—no rhythm—but I figure now is not the time to tell him that Neal Peart is a pale imitator of Art Blakey's dropping-bombs style of syncopation. Then again, I'm a pale imitator of paleness myself, so I just say, *You know who hates Rush?* Heather's other brother and friend have rejoined us, and with the threat of violence that had once been so close now removed, we're bestest friends and they're hanging on my every word, sorry to have doubted me and my skin and *Heeb* ain't great but it's a whole lot better than—

Who hates Rush? Tim asks, eyes wide, genuinely curious.

I tease the moment a beat, then answer sagely: *Chicks hate Rush.*

We do a donut in the gravel, pulling out, Marc musing, *Chicks hate Rush . . . Words of fuckin' wisdom.*

I see Heather for a few weeks after that, her brothers singing "Hava Nagilah" whenever they answer the door, all smiles on their faces and proffered beers in their hands. When she consents to sleep with me that spring before going off to some risible state college in the Midwest, I fuck her with a condom, whose wrapped center, moments before, and unseen by her, I have pierced with a fine sewing needle.

You always remember your first.

CHAPTER XIV

THE CROSSING

By 1990, five years out of Coppin, I was enrolled in the nearly all-white Towson State University in suburban Baltimore and had severed my gossamer ties with the black world.* Everyone at the Sheraton, where I still worked after four years while attending college part-time, thought I was white. When the NAACP convention was held in Baltimore, thousands of black people from all over the country filled the hotel's suites and dining rooms for breakfast, lunch, and dinner. On day one, one of my friends, a pockmarked, ribald fellow waiter with a waterfront accent, laid an empty soup bowl on the floor as his station filled with conventioneers. He whistled, just loud enough to hear, and snapped his fingers in the direction of his diners as though coaxing a blue heeler, *c'mere boy*, and with a wink to me, *might as well make 'em feel at home.* I chuckled like a lunatic, and was still laughing when I saw my Aunt Fran—my grandmother's niece—a tenured professor of European studies, fluent in French, German,

---

*I had amassed a whopping twenty-four credits during those years, including the ones I had transferred from Coppin.

and Italian, raising a tentative hand from her table to greet me. I had spent those Thanksgivings we did not partake of the Horn & Horn's bounty at the table of my Aunt Fran and her mother, Nellie, who was my grandmother's sister-in-law. My friend said, upon seeing that outstretched hand, *them bufers at your table need you.*

Not my station, I replied. The convention lasted a week, and I called in sick every day after the first. By this point, it was nothing personal, strictly business. There were one or two black waiters at the restaurant, but for the most part, blacks were dishwashers, busboys, porters. Some of them would glower at me as, puffed up with asinine pride, I walked past them on my way to serve whitey in the dining room. I heard the mutters of, *he one of them high-yella niggers, think he cute*, but I feigned a lethean superiority. I was at the top of the menial labor food chain, making more than my father had as the managing editor of the *Baltimore Afro-American*, and nobody was going to blow it for me. Granted, my job did not consist of interviewing El-Hajj Malik El Shabazz, or Miles Davis, but of little more than bearing food to humans, the terminus of my labors septic tanks and sewers.

I was still close with my father, but our daily lives were separate now that I was on my own; Stefan was gone, and Khari—having moved in with a friend of his from middle school, a boy whose family felt that they could provide a more reasonable environment for him than the squalor of The House—was in high school, an equable and well-liked black boy in a mostly black public school in northern Baltimore. Good. I was white now, all the way white—gone were the days of picking and choosing based on the vicissitudes of schools, girls, neighborhoods. There was no turning back, despite the close calls, of which there were many.

Sitting on the steps of a friend's house in the white working-class Baltimore neighborhood of Canton, I saw a girl of about ten, leading her baby sister, a round seraph who could not have been more than four, by the hand down the sidewalk. These two were fresh from the Franklin Mint—plumped full of the rosy-cheeked goodness and cascading curls that America beams from televisions and milk cartons alike. The older girl suddenly stopped across the narrow residential street and turned her sister round to face me. I smiled. She bent a little over her sister's shoulder and pointed at me.

Nigger daddy, she instructed the tyke . . . *nigger* . . . *daddy*, once more, in order that the girl not forget the lesson. I stared at my shoes, unable to muster any real anger. She was right, after all, an inchoate social anthropologist, trained well and early. She could have said, "nigger," or "nigger mommy," but she had adroitly triangulated, in seconds, who I was, down to the specifics of my parentage.

I say that I could not muster any real anger, but that is only partly true. For a few moments on those steps I fantasized peeling the panties from around her formless hips while her cherubic baby sister, her mechanic/air-conditioning repairman/cop/stevedore father, and her bedsit-due-to-morbid-obesity mother watched on in prostrate horror as I fucked her—at first gingerly, in deference to her age and unaccommodating anatomy—and then ad libitum—my cock sheathed in ground glass. I quickly disabused myself of this wretched fantasy, as the logistics of such an enterprise seemed certain to cause as much physical distress to the raper as to the raped.

———◆———

I had been living with my girlfriend Melissa, a modern dancer, who like Heather was from the white working-class suburb of Baltimore (Dundalk!), for two and a half years. She was sweet, freckled, full of rousing curves, and we were hopelessly in love, or at least we had been in the beginning. I was nineteen when we met, she a year younger, and we moved in together soon after and far too young. Numerous affairs and attempts to "find ourselves" had left us snarling and mistrustful. She cared for me in the way I supposed mothers cared for their sons: she cooked my meals, scrubbed my clothes, made sure my hair was cut and my teeth were brushed. I became infantilized, and boys did not fuck their mothers, this much about the alien transaction I knew.

Melissa had attended the Baltimore School for the Arts high school, a *Fame*-like academy known for the moral laxity of its female students.* Only Catholic school girls were rumored to be easier lays. Though Melissa was only the second girl I had ever been with, and my first girlfriend, within a year all I could think about was the pussy I wasn't getting. A bird in hand, in my case, was not worth all that missing bush.

Melissa had seen and, bless her guileless soul, been corrupted by some bromidic film, *Summer Lovers,* which featured an impossibly beautiful Daryl Hannah, another woman, and some straight-from-central-casting Adonis, all of whom lolled nakedly about the Cycladic Isles in various configurations of coition. In an attempt to stave off our own inevitable demise, she suggested we take a trip to Greece.

My mother's brief abduction of me as an infant notwithstanding, I had never been on a plane before and found air travel, which I'd thought only for the rich, thrilling. Melissa and many other passengers were terrified at the landings, turbulence, and takeoffs, but I sneered at the feeble ninnies, relishing every airborne event. Melissa sat on the aisle, beside me, and a Greek boy of eleven or so, who spoke no English, flanked me by the window. I did not, *could not* sleep during the flight. As we banked in a wide motion, the jet squaring itself to the runway at Athens Airport, Melissa squeezed my hand

---

*Her classmates were the rapper Tupac Shakur, the actress Jada Pinkett, and my first love, Susan Berger.

until I thought my knuckles would fragment. The boy with the window seat (how I had coveted it!) snapped down the window shade in a huff, a sham bit of bravado by which he hoped to convey a *Bah! If you've seen one landing you've seen 'em all!* but I saw the sweat on his upper lip, and the way he turned from the view.

I had paid my $500 fare, and I wanted the whole show, the sizzle as well as the steak. I leaned across the boy and authoritatively unclosed the shade. He looked at me, as we alighted upon the Athenian exurbs, with such barely concealed terror that I held out my hand to him, touching down upon foreign soil with both my mitts kneaded into an arthritic pulp.

As Melissa and I shuffled between lurching ferries and whitewashed pensiones, teetering beneath gravid backpacks, something unusual happened. In fact, it would happen so frequently, in the midst of the exigencies of first-time budget travelers—*how many drachmas to the dollar? is that the gay beach, the gay nude beach, or the super gay, super nude party beach?*—that I almost didn't notice. I was even mildly bemused the first dozen or so times I was mistaken for—well, anyone but an American.

<hr />

It happened everywhere we went. When we ran into Italian travelers, crammed into a ship's fo'c'sle, they spoke Italian to me; when we drank *metaxa* on the beach with rowdy French teenagers, they prattled on to me in the language of diplomacy, reverting to pidgin English when addressing my lily-white girlfriend. Naturally, I understood not a word of what they were saying, but my imbecilic nodding probably gave them the impression I was following right along. My typically American vexation, of the *Jesus, doesn't anybody speak English in this country?* variety softened into an appreciation of the fact that, as usual, I was being defined by others, but this time the definition was broad, encompassing a continent. I came from a place where I had been offered two options: black or white. Europe, with its millennial history of mongrel hordes and cross-pollination, saw me as one of its own and offered me a third way.

A good mimic, I picked up a few rudimentary Greek catchphrases and tossed them about cavalierly, watching anxiously for the patronizing smiles or corrective measures that never came. The freedom was exhilarating. For once, my lover—that prize of America's corn and wheat and milk and honey—was the outcast, the empty tourist with pasty skin, broiled to a brilliant cerise, and I was the international boulevardier, made yet more swarthy by the Aegean sun and jocose by peasant wines. I was every bit as clueless as Melissa when it came to customs, protocol, or directions, but for the very first time I was *given the benefit of the doubt*, without any machinations on my part.

As a child, it had always been my dream to escape with Stefan on one of his yearly sorties. Having met his mother just that once, I knew beyond a doubt that I would not have been required nor permitted to contribute a penny of my own for food and upkeep—I was family—but the (then) three-hundred-dollar airfare and Europe remained elusive as hen's teeth. To buoy my spirits during the school years, Stefan filled many afternoons prepping me for my first world travels. I was furnished, on the steps of my Mt. Royal apartment building, with a couple of phrases in case we got separated in Parisian back alleys (the most I can remember is *plus ta merde*), and taught, legs bowed and bent, to ride an invisible motorcycle that lay gassed and waiting in the barn outside his mother's castle, *left-hand clutch, first-gear down, then hook the shifter under your boot* . . .

Years later, I visited Stefan in Cap d'Ail, in the South of France. Somewhat estranged from him by 1996, that summer, through the miracle of uncrossed communications, I happened to receive a postcard, or a phone call, I cannot remember which, apprising me of his whereabouts. Just a few months hence, me and my then girlfriend Pamela—a leggy blonde coed from the University of Maryland—were slated to visit (again, for I was nothing if not a creature of habit) the Greek

Isles,* so it was settled upon—twenty years after the subject was first broached—that I would at last join Stefan on his home turf. We had not seen each other since my last days at Coppin and his last at City, and Stefan now had a wife, an infant daughter, and a pied-à-terre a baguette's throw from Monaco.

I should have known something was wrong the moment I arrived.

Stefan picked us up at the Nice train station and proceeded to whisk us through winding boulevards and precipitous mountain passes without regard for the "lesser" gears on his battered Saab, until, at long last, on a claustrophobic lane brimming with Vespas and reclusive cinema stars, he violently sheared the side mirror of some dilatory motorist who had attempted to evacuate a parking space at a ponderous fifty miles per hour. We arrived at our first destination, Stefan's "yacht," battered and carsick.

We boarded this dilapidated vessel, which looked like the abandoned set of a cheesy adult film from the (early)

---

*I have never been particularly adventurous in my recreational pursuits. Travel had always been such a financial hardship, a luxury, that I did not suffer the romantic notions of "discovering" new places and peoples. To my dyspeptic mind, I had accumulated enough information about "people" to determine that I cared for them not a bit; and the "places" to which I could afford to travel were either squalid Oriental slums or irksome, student-abroad "party islands." If I hated people with a gentle simmer, I hated "party people" with a rolling boil.

seventies, as the sun set over the Riviera. Suitably impressed, my girlfriend *oohed* and *ahhed,* but I knew that with Stefan, one could shod a centipede and still need to be wary of the falling of the "other shoe"—bon vivant though he had always been, he had also just as certainly been a hustler, with as much black Baltimore as Grenache in his veins.

As I leaned over the bow and watched the glitterati tend to their vulgar (which is not to suggest that they were not impressive, and beautiful) floating behemoths moored along the docks, and started to ask, for what must have been the fifth time in as many minutes, what endeavors provided Stefan this existence, I noticed a small motorized skiff buzzing toward us from the docks. Stefan squinted, and walked to the lee. The two Frenchmen in the dinghy shouted with raised fists and nasal bellows up to Stefan, who purred calmly back in silken tones, like Pepe le Pew to a feline in estrus. The brief contretemps ended with Stefan's suggestion that we vacate the boat as quickly as possible, a recommendation made only *after* he had asked me, smiling, sotto voce through clenched teeth moments prior, whether I could "float" him the sum of three or four thousand dollars. While this was hardly my vision of two lads racing across the French countryside on motorbikes, or traipsing through antediluvian castles in the mist, I was at last with my oldest best friend, in Europe, beneath a scarlet dying sun in the South of France, on a yacht.

By the end of our stay with Stefan and his Norwegian, nearly translucent wife, Liv, I began to understand the prehistory of Stefan's racial oblivion, which had been forming, like sedimentary layers, since childhood. On beaches, I watched as menopausal women with floppy hats and dimpled arms tottered over to his chaise and with their free hands (whose twin was curled tightly around a gelid *noilly prat*) offer scraps of paper which, to my slack-jawed amazement, he was invited to autograph. The first time this happened (and it did frequently), he paused midconversation, signed the dowager's paper, and turned to me with a sigh, *I'm sorry . . . this happens all the time*, to which, after years of remove from his stultifying shadow, I asked in a froth: *Who the fuck are you supposed to be?* He was about to give me some blithe, demurring answer when a dark-skinned black man with a high-top fade, and a pair of cerise Speedos around his flanks, ambled over. They chatted in French, and Stefan introduced me. The man flashed a set of teeth so harmoniously arranged and pearlescent that they might have been commissioned by Steinway, and began speaking to me in a slightly compromised American accent. He asked where I was from, and when I told him, and subsequently made mention of the university I was attending, the University of Maryland at College Park, he exclaimed, *That's where I went!*

I asked—though by this point I was somewhat be-numbed to the presence of these two (three, if you were so inclined to count me—but I was a guest) Maryland

black men lounging on the beach in the world's most ex-
clusive principality—what line of work this gentleman
was in. He said, *I'm a musician.* I must have nodded
rather too nonchalantly, causing Liv to admonish, *That's
Haddaway—you don't know who Haddaway is?* She then
hummed a bit of something, which could have been considered not unlike music, depending on the laxity of one's
definition, and the corners of my mouth curled in recognition. I'm sure the ersatz "musician" thought, despite
my imprimis failure to comprehend his considerable talents, that I had now, by dint of Liv's gentle prompting,
come round to a sensible appreciation of who he was, my
puckered dimples and flashing eyeteeth approbation of
his status. Not quite. You see, I recognized that tune, and
at the risk of infecting you, dear reader, who may be
blessedly unfamiliar with the oeuvre of Mr. Haddaway
and his four-minute-and-twelve-second malaise that Europe and homosexual America had deigned a "hit," my
smile was in recollection of the song as it had become
known to me, an ironical American, as the soundtrack
that sent two comedians from television's *Saturday Night
Live* caroming wildly off the bodies of horrified females,
week after week.

He took his leave of us, but not before inviting us
onto his boat that weekend; despite my knowledge to the
contrary, I felt that a god must have intervened in human
affairs and made our departure date that Friday. As his
ass, in its scant raiment, twitched away down the beach,

I could not help but wonder why Stefan had not asked *that* rich cocksucker for the monies with which to free his *Grampus*.

Truly, Europe had no prejudices: Stefan, without visible means of support, and his friend Haddaway, lacking discernible talent, were much more than niggers. It occurred to me that perhaps it was better to be a nigger in America, with blood and music and history soaking through to the bedrock, than a gewgaw in Europe, a freak.

CHAPTER XV

REBEL WITHOUT A PAUSE

Once I had beheld the miracle of cable television, the constricting polemics of UHF and VHF were so many cataracts obscuring the plenary abundance behind their milky haze. In the early nineties, I was finally blessed with the gift of that endless dial, the freely exposed nipples and brandished profanities, oafish public access, jetsam programming crammed onto airwaves so that the viewer would never again have to enter the nival barren wasteland of "off the air." I watched as an adult as I had read as a child, which is to say *comprehensively*, and without prejudice. Senate hearings were scrutinized with the same avid attention as *Fawlty Towers*. Working nights meant that I (often literally) got the dog's breakfast of programming—"Book TV" lectures by James Baldwin, documentaries about the Black Panthers, eight hours of *Shoah*, lurid and lubricated assignations with Cinemax, and that shrill obscenity known as MTV. A dilettante's wet dream made manifest.

Freed somewhat by my travels from America's racialist *durance vile*, I nonetheless remained philosophically unmoored, though I knew that my own churlish, reductive nature made the movement known as "political correctness" an unlikely ontological fit. A tangential benefit of that enfeebling cultural diktat was the justifiable *anger* that smoldered at its core. Before naïf coeds had farcically ventured forth into Ivy League quads, their candles inhumed in Dixie cups in droll resolve to "take back the night," the spark of discontent that made political correctness necessary was fed by people every bit (nay, more) as marginalized as I had imagined myself to be. Those who did not have the luxury of hiding behind ambiguous skin, who had suffered—not dodged, nor hyperrealized—instances of real racism, sexism, overt discrimination. Some of these people found their way onto television, where they made lunatic assertions regarding the state of the union in the most heated, fantastical, and, somewhat incongruously, *cogent* manner I had yet heard. I was held in thrall as the Minister Louis Farrakhan ceaselessly dabbed at his fulgent brow with a silken handkerchief and enumerated the litany of crimes and deceptions the Jews (and the white man in general) had perpetrated against the black man. I knew that this man was quite obviously and irreducibly insane, just as I also understood him to make perfect sense.

Reductive reasoning had always appealed to me as a fixed and resolute bearing in the choppy sea of my formless identity. In the same way I had chosen white over black to the exclusion of all other racial configurations, my dialectical tendencies across the board left no room for subtlety or shades of grey. When the "minister" averred to his fawning claque that Jews controlled the media, could I disagree? I had, in my early years spent before the television, made note of the homogenously Semitic names of the writers, directors, producers, and even stars of myriad shows, from the gritty urban fare of *Good Times* (Norman Lear), to the pastoral America of Mayberry, North Carolina, via *The Andy Griffith Show* (Aaron Ruben), to the bland national "truths" of network news presided over by Ted Koppel, Don Hewitt, Mike Wallace. Coincidence? A result of tenacious hard work and a cultural tendency toward scholarship and the arts? Or a sinister plot to control the very nature of information and its dissemination so that the world might be trued to a Jewish sensibility, at the same time that Jews lamented their past persecutions and present-day exclusion from the very "mainstream" that, in fact, they had created and defined. Jews who had manufactured in their movie studios and advertising lairs not only those idylls of snub-nose nymphs and square-jawed straight shooters, that world which tantalized while doubting me, but also that other world, that *Jewish* world of people who sort of looked like me, laughed like me, kvetched like me, but regarded me with a suspicion unequaled by even the most niveous gentile. The rebukes I had suffered (or felt that I had suffered, and what is the difference to the partially unhinged?) at the hands of my "chosen" people found relief in that manqué calypso singer's orotund sermons, and comfort too in the reductive semiotics of one Dr. Frances Cress Welsing.

I lack the grey matter required to give even the most cursory exegesis of her theories, but those facets that struck me, as though with a diamond bullet, I (mis?) understood thusly:

White racism is a biological imperative effectuated by white Europeans as a systematic attempt to prevent their genetic annihilation by the global majority of the world's darker peoples, whose genes, being dominant, would necessarily eclipse recessive white genes. Wham, bam, no more honkies. Of course. It made sense from the first *what are you?* lobbed my way by a dubious father, to the last *nigger daddy* prod into my heart by ogling tykes. Fear, not ignorance; racism is not about ignorance, Dr. Welsing explained; it's about *knowledge* (originally it had been about economics, but since 1864 fear had stepped into the vacuum). The fact that some knowledge is ineffable does not make it any less valid. Whites *knew* that there would be no blending of the races without an ending of the races, and they had been on a pretty long winning streak. (American trope number twenty-seven: don't mess with success.) Prehension of their tenuous genetic majority limited, in a very real way, how much of a melting pot this nation would ever truly allow itself to become. Watching Dr. Welsing on whatever low-rent cable show (*Tony Brown's Journal?*) she happened to visit, the rightness of her assertions struck me as undeniable, her logic inexorable. White people were not inherently evil (which would have been *my* jumping-off point), they were doing what any species would do when faced with extinction. Rat. In. Corner.

I scared white people. The possibility that they trembled before the tincture of my jism was a new concept for me. I was the annihilator of a race of cowards instead of the annihilator of just myself. There was no biracial, no mulatto—just black and white in an amaranthine war, any compromise to whitey a defeat. I was not mixed, I was black. Not ascribed as such, *by them*, in an attempt to keep me from the loins of their maidens, and the chairs of their boardrooms, but described as such *by me*, as the one who held the power of their destruction like a swollen purple trident between my legs.

Once we (black people) began to understand the foundations and, just as important, the *definition* of racism—a definition that had heretofore been sanitized and etiolated until it was nothing but a shrill attempt to induce guilt, which in any event worked only on pseudo-liberals and television networks—we could mount a defensive. I don't recall how, but I sure liked the ring of all that other stuff!

Dr. Welsing went on, in captivatingly lurid detail, about the ways in which race had leached into our collective subconscious through symbols. Cigarettes, white and puny, were called "fags," while cigars, fat and long and brown, conveyed power. Good stuff, but shit gets deeper. The cigar conveyed said power because it was the white man's castration and subsequent consumption of the genetically dominant black man and his power, much like the cannibals of the South Seas ate their enemies' hearts so that they would be made stronger.* Okay, some of this may seem spurious, but I hadn't heard anything that described the phenomena of racism in a way that seemed rational—and I knew, having been a racist my whole life, that racism was exceedingly rational. And I was a sucker for a good simile. Given that my previous, fatuous decisions regarding my own racial determination had been made amid a calculation of pros and cons weighed as scrupulously as gold dust, my avowal of my own blackness would have to be just as ponderously undertaken.

Along with Dr. Welsing, and an endless loop of *Eyes on the Prize* (which seemed to constitute the black cable network BET's sole programming), there was the music. The soundtrack to the slew of faces and philosophies that had been barred from my history books and college lectures—unknown notables like Stokely Carmichael, H. Rap Brown, Bobby Seale, and Malcolm X—was the sound of Armageddon set to sirens, carefully arranged snippets of agitprop and black nationalist manifesto, all at a hundred beats per minute.†

---

*I was later, in a seriocomic vein, to attempt the same sort of extrapolation on the subject of white chocolate. I reasoned that the white man created white chocolate because he couldn't stand the fact that something so delicious was black.

†I have not forgotten that I had grown up with a black nationalist who could have told me more about the black power movement and its players

I had always hated rap music. "Raising my hands in the air (like I just didn't care)" was not a form of lyrical inspiration I could take to heart, and the monotonous beat, lack of musicianship (or music), and trite subject matter were all just further examples of the low bar black America, like a race of pygmy limbo dancers, had set for itself. But then, at the turn of the decade, something shifted. Public Enemy had a sound that was insistent and could not be denied, their densely packed lyrics the recondite equal of any Dylan epic (not that I listened to him—some lessons took longer than others to take hold). I heard them deliver, in a basso-baritone call to arms, names like Joanne Chesimard, Huey P. Newton, the aforementioned Farrakhan, toe-tapping descriptions and strident denunciations of the white man and his role in the destruction of the black race, but also (and just as important for me) the black man's complicity in that four-hundred-year-old minuet. The group's leader, Chuck D, had concisely avowed that their music was about *beats for your feets and rhymes for your mind.* Not a dancer, I was thus able to channel all of the energies Mr. D had intended to vitiate throughout my poles concertedly into my cerebellum.

The musical and cultural popularization of black nationalist/separatist/power/protest thought proved to be just the teaspoon of sugar I needed to help my poison,

---

than any book or tepid documentary, but we take our medicines the same way we take our poisons: when we are ready.

blackness, go down smooth and sweet. We were not a bunch of sodden Negroes, heads bowed, waiting for our piece of the American pie at segregated lunch counters; we had a youth culture drawing its own lines of engagement. I began reading the intellectual giants of black thought—James Baldwin, Frantz Fanon, Charles Henrik Clarke, Amiri Baraka—fusing them with the crumbling Grecian foundations of my slapped-together education. From Baldwin, lyrical indignation; Fanon, semiotic ire; Clarke, painstaking scholarship; Baraka, sublime rage.

As I began my journeyman apprenticeship into his world, my father and I grew closer. I lectured him one afternoon on the merits of the film *Malcolm X,* even prodding him to see it, after which he good-naturedly snapped, *Why would I go see somebody pretending to be my friend?* My new hero (unlike the untouchable John Lennon or Woody Allen) was right next to me, in the singular, gently rumpled form of Ralph Matthews Jr., my father. Here was a primary source, my very own Schomburg Center, and it was with an avid, if also delinquent, rapacity that I remade his acquaintance. I had always known him and loved him, to be sure, but it had been a conditional love, predicated upon his remaining in the shadows, he in his world, me in mine. He filtered all of my "new" interests (for despite the faddish renaissance of nineties black culture, those were nothing but recycled tropes going back as far as Marcus Garvey) with and for me, decrying the "quacks" (Farrakhan) and commending the "soldiers" (Malcolm X,

LeRoi Jones—he never could get used to calling him by his Africanized name, Amiri). He was bemused by the wildly vacillating pendulum of my identity, and, I suppose, after a lifetime of self-denial, it is no surprise, nor is it an excuse, that I did go a trifle overboard.

Now a "black" militant of sorts, my white appearance remained unchanged. I made haughty pronouncements like *Black people can't be racist*,* because of the institutional nature of racism, or theorized that Martin Luther King Jr. had been a contrapuntal Uncle Tom Negro leader whose effectiveness lay in the fact that he was the lesser of two black evils, more palatable to the white establishment than, say, Malcolm X, Huey P. Newton, or Kwame Toure, né Stokely Carmichael, whose "other cheeks" would not be turned. My father patiently, and with great good humor, taught me much of what he knew and corrected much of what I thought I knew. He, of course, hated white people, though for entirely different reasons than I. He hated them for excluding his people from the basic rights of man; I hated them for making me choose between my father and my mother, though this awareness came late, and is still in many ways tenebrous. I had chosen my mother (her whiteness), though she had aban-

---

*This opinion has not been mitigated in any way. Black people can be *prejudiced*, and can hate white people, but these antipathies lack the power to deny whites housing, employment, or equal treatment under the law. Racism is, in the American context at least, an institution, and not a sentiment.

doned me, and ignored my father (his blackness), though he had not.

During these endless collegiate years (I would spend over a decade in pursuit of a bachelor's degree), my friends and girlfriends remained the same motley assortment of white liberals. I remember taking one blond vixen, Molly, who had plenary breasts and boyish hips, to a showing of *Malcolm X* and after she had collapsed, sobbing into my arms, blubbering, *Why did people have to be like that?* I stroked her flaxen mane and whispered to myself, *There, there, blue-eyed devil,* until I could assuage her guilt and re-dress her crimes the only way I knew how, her apologies screamed into a pillow, her platinum snatch raised high in the air, backing into, then away, then into, my cock. It was not my forty acres and a mule, but it was a start.

I would now hold court among my white liberal friends, explaining to them how racist they "really were." I was an asshole, but in my defense I was nearly always shocked at how little I had to scratch the surface of a lib-eral before the racist underneath shone through, their re-pressed views unearthed like silt stirred to the top of a crystal-clear lagoon. To my theatrical but no less impas-sioned shakedowns they would offer replies of *I could to-tally marry a black man, but it would kill my parents,* or, *The Irish had it tough, too, when they came to America.* The only incontrovertible proof of whether a person is, or is not, a racist is whether he/she would marry a black per-son, or care whether a family member does. (The old taboo used to be fucking, but since marriage is foremost about money, and fucking a black person—or a black man at any rate—is now merely "cultural exploration" for many white girls, part of the liberal to-do list on par with a semester of slavish lesbianism or the acquisition of a trite, vaguely oriental tattoo, marriage is the last frontier.) My favorite trope of liberal Aryan American mothers and fathers remains: *We just worry about how hard it will be for your kids . . . not everyone is as understanding as we are, dear.**

Laughably, having buried my true identity for so long, and now, with so much effort, embraced my history, my father's legacy, the richness of my tapestry, the second and most vexing aspect of my "blackness" occurred: *no one believed me.*

I told these same friends, to no avail, of my exploits in my old neighborhood, the guns and drugs and the adventures of my father. But by the early nineties the wigger had been born, and I was just another in a growing line that began with Vanilla *I'm from the streets, word to your mother* Ice and would culminate, by the end of the decade, with *Hi, my name is* Slim Shady. So cloaked was I in the habiliment of the Jewish intellectual, I was refused all other garb: no kente cloth, no dashiki, no Fubu track suit. I was sentenced to being white.

---

*Come to think of it, I suppose it is a *bit* trying for the kids, depending upon their constitutions.

CHAPTER XVI

THE HEART OF THE WORLD

In first grade, along with my classmates, I was asked
to pick a nation (excluding America), research, and complete a report on it, all while bedizened in the native garb
of that peregrine land. I settled upon the cheerless Soviet
annex Yugoslavia, precisely because I knew that no one
else would. I was happy to sit back and watch the other
six-year-olds grab at each other's throats and rend *The
World and Its Peoples* textbooks from their neighbors'
hands in a colonialist furor—*I picked Alaska first!*

I scoured my father's fractional *Encyclopedia
Britannica*—oddly, though there was no "D" or "L," the
"Y" volume was present, its spine uncracked and pyretic
trim unmarred, and copied every word verbatim. When I
finished at somewhere close to eleven the evening before
my report was due, I shook the writer's cramp from my
left hand and plopped in front of the TV in anticipation
of my father's arrival.* When he got home two hours
later, as Doc Severinson fellated his trumpet over the

---

*Karen and Elijah do not figure in this remembrance, though I don't
doubt their propinquity.

credits of *The Tonight Show*, I yawned and informed him that we'd better get on it, as we had less than seven hours to fabricate a bespoke, traditional Yugoslavian ensemble, the necessity of which, I, in my amnesiac childishness, had neglected to apprise my father of until that very moment. (In my defense, I had scrupulously marked the page in the Britannica where the thumbnail-sized picture of a Yugoslavian in full raiment resided, in order that he would not puzzle his head over matters of design.) After a thirteen-hour day at the office, he was not happy. At first, he tried to impart a well-needed object lesson of the *this'll teach you not to put things off till the last minute*, but he knew that would be wholly wasted, as I had witnessed his heavy-lidded escapes from the apartment at nine, ten, eleven A.M. during the workweek, and the utility company's serial interruptions of our electricity owing to the dilatory nature of his payments; he must have surmised (correctly) that he would have had better luck pushing water up a hill with a rake than trying to undo years of his example.

By some miracle, a sewing machine was retrieved from the depths of a closet floor, and we began our fabrication. Bleary-eyed by the time we'd figured out how to get the thread onto the bobbin, we both gulped Maxwell House instant coffee larded with Carnation instant creamer and sugar until we were as giddy as hopped-up truckers on an interstate run. With wistful stolidity, he hacked apart one of his dress shirts, dismantled a pair of gabardine knit pants, and violated a corduroy suit vest until we had the necessary material. Hunched over the sewing machine—mists of cigarette smoke shrouding his labors—he pieced together, stitching his fingers as often as fabric, a suit that to my bloodshot eyes looked every bit as good as the one the yokel Sarajevan from the Britannica was wearing. My culottes were stapled as often as they were sewn; my vest would brook no actual movement, lest its artifice come undone; and my tunic was tucked fairly into my lederhosen. He also made a pair of shoes. Breaking two needles on the Singer, he shod me in two metamorphosed vinyl place mats, their appearance slightly more elfin than Slavic. As the sun came up, I awoke to the sight of his grizzled countenance pulling the last safety pin from between his lips and saying gently, *Ready for school, buddy?*

Movement—once clothed—a precarious endeavor at best, he carried me to the car, placed me in the reclined front seat, and drove me to school. He waited while I stammered (neither a stitch nor seam came undone!) through my report and, begging the teacher off with the excuse of a doctor's appointment, returned us both to home and bed seemingly moments later. That recollection brings with it an eidetic chill, as it has always been accompanied by another image of my father.

From my kindergarten desk, I often daydreamed out

the window, beyond which was a wall below which I could not see, save for the raised, crenulated jaws of a bulldozer that ate into a pile of overflowing soil. The jaws went to and fro, until one morning, as I mechanically sung "My Country, 'Tis of Thee," I imagined, just as we got to the lyric *land where my fathers died*, that behind that wall was a cemetery, and into those holes would go my father, and go soon. I don't know how I conflated those abstract images and that existential snippet, but I cannot shake the image of my father bent over the Singer, his mouth studded with pins, and his commission to the grave.

———————•◆•———————

Somehow, perhaps as a ship rights itself in the middle of a storm, the black me and the white me came to a truce, brokered in large part by New York City. In my early thirties, as far along in my education as I ever would be, and as well versed in the intricacies of the Baltimore/Washington restaurant industry as befitted someone of my moony aspirations, I moved to that awesome and horrible and magnificent New Amsterdam and found not America but Europe redivivus. Hasidic pamphleteers accosted me with certitude, *may I speak to you? are you Jewish?* and Popi's in bodegas sold me Snapples in Spanish. Fujianese kids and Italian greaseballs played handball alongside dreadlocked rastas in the Alphabet, and we all bundled against the frangible cold and ignored

one another, or else wilted, cursing in the fetid heat.* I
was free and easy about my makeup, in direct proportion
to society's disinterest. I knocked off the fatuous talk of
revolution and devils and simply stated—on those infrequent occasions when someone asked—that my father
was black and my mother was white. New York made it
easy, though I recognized that while it is not America,
Baltimore most certainly is. New York was an eight-mile
gumbo of ultracondensed multiculturalism, a freak, a
one-off—the real America lay in the event horizon past
125th Street, and in the frontiers of Nostrand Avenue,
where a brandished wallet reminded me in nineteen,
hollow-pointed ways that I had not simply imagined my
racist America in Baltimore, nor had to live the worst of
it. New York, Los Angeles, Johannesburg—*er, sorry*—
Boston, these were politically correct dream states that
had nothing to do with America. I laughed inwardly as
the "evolved" denizens of these cosmopolises refuted me
with their slavish obiter dicta that racism was "over." My
battles had taught me to walk away from (when not tun-
ing in to) lunatics, liberals, and conservatives—a redun-
dancy, I'll admit—but with every national election or

---

*Rather than regurgitate the hoary (though arguably correct) chestnut
that "New York is the greatest city in the world!" I would fain ask where
else in the free world are citizens asked to endure, as a matter of course,
streets and subways filled with rivers of human waste, and extortionate
rent in aid of inhospitable slum-dwelling.

hurricane, I was regrettably validated. The real America was as segregated as ever, with money and class (rather the lack of it) becoming the new "black."

For the first protracted period of my life, I found myself in a luxurious racial stasis. To be sure, all my daily endeavors were an unqualified failure: thirteen years in pursuit of a bachelor's degree; a penury of forty-seven thousand dollars in student loans; a phalanx of agents, managers, and risible Hollywood studio executives, all of whom assured me that if only my material weren't so "dark," great success in their glycerin racket loomed; and an undesired, if necessary—so that I might ameliorate somewhat the pangs in my belly and the gnawing demands of that previously mentioned colossus of scholastic fealty—mastery of the food and beverage arts. I was that bunioned cliché, the writer/waiter/bartender/maître d'. But at least I had come close to answering most of my life's Great Questions.

Close, however, counts only in horseshoes and hand grenades.

———•———

Nearly thirty years after my premonition of his death, in the spring of 2002, my father underwent a quintuple bypass and died on the operating table. Forty-three seconds later, his heart was revived between the massaging palms of a cardiovascular surgeon at Washington

Hospital Center, though he would spend the next fort-night in a coma. Immediately after the surgery, which had been planned with the exhaustiveness of a long-awaited Mediterranean cruise, his wife called me to con-sider what sort of final arrangements Ralph might have wanted. Scarcely the night before, already sick with a vi-olent flu, I had called my dad to tell him that I loved him and to wish him good luck.

Did you hear me? I asked, after I'd declared the for-mer. Over the months before, I had been told not to worry—everybody from David Letterman to Larry King had gotten a "zipper"; it was the new rhinoplasty. I waited, jaws clacking from ague, for his reply to my ad-mission, which felt like a flood of ice water over an ab-scessed tooth. I had revealed too much . . . *told,* not shown—the bane of good writing and healthy relation-ships. Us Matthews Men didn't blubber on about love and death. After what seemed like forever, but was likely the lull between two heartbeats, he replied: *Right back at you, kid.*

Even staring down the barrel of his own death, *cool* prevailed.

During those first few days, when his dying seemed like a much safer bet than his survival, I was not allowed to see him, though my fever had broken. I was stuck in New York, with a heart full of impotent hurt, and a head full of unanswered questions. *Right back at you?* Weak and ashen, I cursed myself and our "cool," and despaired that I had not had a lifetime of tousled heads and arms around shoulders and stubbly kisses on cheeks or the knowledge of who my mother had been or what he had seen in her or her in him or not in me. My father was the only person I ever met who had known my mother.

As fantastical as it may seem, I had always been relatively incurious about the specifics of my mother and her history. Certainly, my friends and girlfriends (for whom the resolution of my "mother" riddle likely represented the surcease of a legion of untold miseries) had expressed muffled incredulity in regard to my disinterest, supposing no doubt that the wound was simply too deep and putrefacted to be examined, and that after so much denial and so many years, peeling away the protective gauze was best left to the world of Viennese psychiatrists, strapping orderlies, and leather restraints.

If the old man took his answers with him, I would have nobody to blame but myself. *Cool*, he was, but if my life hitherto was any litmus, cool was one thing I could safely say I was not.

Here is the hard evidence regarding my mother that I was in possession of after thirty-seven years:

- Her name was Robin Kahn.
- She was from the Midwest.
- She was from a rich Jewish family.

- She flew me to Israel when I was an infant.
- Her grandfather donated a library or something to the city of Minneapolis.
- She lived in Israel after I was born.

I made a date to "interview" my father during the first week of July 2005. Through the phone, I could hear the stertorous *click* of the oxygen hose, which had been insinuated into his nostrils for nearly every moment of the last few years of his crawling recovery. He cautioned me against too much optimism. *You have to remember, of the few memories I have of that time, few are pleasant. Don't sweat it,* I said, *we'll see what happens. Just do me a favor?*

Yup?

Don't croak before I get there.

Such a good son.

I packed a valise with clean skivvies and a book (Hubert Selby Jr.'s *The Room*) for the nearly four-hour train ride, and popped a melatonin as a nostrum against chronic insomnia, which could not be indulged this evening as my train left Pennsylvania Station at ten thirty-five the next morning (practically the middle of my night). I proceeded to lie abed for hours, wide awake, feeling like Ross Macdonald's fictional detective Lew Archer in the incipient hours after he has resolved, no matter the risk to his personal injury, to see the case through to its solution. This hard-boiled resolve was truncated by the dire realization—which roused me bolt upright, a perfect L—that I had not made a list of questions for my father. I found a moleskin pad filled with virginal pages and began to compose a rudimentary list, along the lines of something a cub reporter might fabricate, a row of neatly penned "hows" and "whys" and "whens." Quite pleased with myself, I poured a finger of single-malt (Bruichladdich) to give angel's wings to the melatonin. While I waited for that speedball to make its effects known, the notion of a little preinvestigative work presented itself as a productive use of time. I powered up my laptop, and realized I would need my mother's exact name, which I had seen only once before, nearly twenty years prior, when I had found it necessary to procure proof of my existence in the form of a Social Security card, which required a priori evidence in the form of a birth certificate. I provided only my father's name and my date of birth, and in return was given an austere wallet-sized computer printout, listing (along with the known information) my mother's name. Now, tumbler of scotch in one hand, I skimmed over high school mash notes written and received, learner's permits, degenerated M-80s (what on earth was I, *am* I, saving those for?) until I found the dog-eared certificate. For the very first time, though it strains even my own credulity to admit, I typed my mother's name, Robin Elinor Kahn, into Google.

———————•◆•———————

I had not really thought this through. Finding her would constitute little more than proof of life on that planet known as my mother. Contact would be something else entirely. I reckoned that, barring an early demise, she would be somewhere in her sixties. Once I discovered her whereabouts, would I have the temerity to initiate contact?

I pictured myself in a rental car on the driveway of some manicured estate, crepitating the gravel under my wheels as I approached her front door. Would she have other kids? If so, they'd be adults, arranged like posies around an oak credenza, aseptic smiles across their faces as they caught a glimpse of our mother's first stab at reproduction, the demo single she abandoned until she found a producer who could give her a hit.

I decided that a face-to-face meeting was out of the question. Hadn't there been a mention of Israel? That bottomless pit was definitely not on my "Places to see before I die" list. Maybe a telephone call. I reminded myself, as the smoky peat singed the lining of my throat, that she may decide she would rather not talk to me. I could already hear the phone nestled back in its cradle with a decisive click. Did I have the brass for a possible *adult* rejection by my mother?

My Google query took 0.14 seconds. It yielded a ton of names to sort through, Kahn being neither quotidian nor exotic. This could take all night. I had no birth date, no locale, no way to winnow the results. Then I saw it, on a Jewish genealogical tree: the Kahn name with some mention of the city of Minneapolis, Minnesota. How many Jews could there have been in Minneapolis? A few spidery branches down the chart was the name Robin Elinor Kahn, born 15 March 1939, in Philadelphia, Pa.

died, 1 May 1977.

I can't be sure. But I know. My mother is dead. My search took 0.14 seconds plus thirty-seven years. The numbers seem right. It says she was married next to her name but that's all it says. Below her name it says she had a child. But that name isn't mine. My body seems to dare me to sleep under the nighttime of this information. Below Robin's name and the child's name is the name of a woman with the same last name, and a birth date with nothing after it. I Google her. There's only one hit, a ritzy Web site for some architecture firm. I type this message—

hello ms. Kahn,

my name is david matthews. my father ralph matthews, married a woman named robin Kahn in 1966, and i was born in 1967. i never met her, and i'm not even sure i'm on the right track, but with what little i have learned from my father (i.e., that my grand-father was a rabbinical scholar/author) and some google snooping, i have somehow found my way to your name. if i'm a) not way off-base, and b) not intruding too much, would it be possible for us to correspond or chat, whichever you're most comfortable with?

i don't mean to open any wounds if there are any, i'm just on a (very belated) journey of self-discovery, of sorts. while people still have their memories and recollections, i'd like to get a sense of my mother and any members of her family who would be willing to share said memories with me. i take it that my mother is no longer living (from aforementioned google snooping), so i guess i'll have to piece together what i can from those who knew her best. my father is getting older, and his memory is of relatively little help, as he has no idea what happened to robin after she went to Israel in '67. i have heard rumors of an assistantship to teddy kollek, but virtually nothing else. i have heard from my father that my maternal grandmother was very kind to me, and in fact spent some time caring for me immediately after my birth.

i am extremely curious about all i've neglected to ask for these past 37 yrs., and hopefully you will find some benefit as well in illuminating for me the other half of where i come from.

best,

david matthews,

—and go to sleep.

I sleep past my train and into the afternoon. Soon my father will call, asking when he should pick me up from D.C.'s Union Station. I can't be bothered to call him back. When I do, I have no idea what I'll tell him. I can't take his cool right now and I can't fake my own.

I check my laptop, and there is a message from an Audrey Kahn, who tells me that Robin was her sister and my mother and that she's been dead for almost thirty years. I call the number she leaves. In a pleasant, nasally voice, she tells me that my mother was profoundly disturbed. She says the word *disturbed* like the admission closes the door on the subject and sticks the key under the mat.

I let her do the talking. She is very nice. She tells me that her family always wondered about me, but thought we would have been too angry with Robin to maintain contact. The hairs at the back of my neck go straight. That's either a lie or a delusion. I know for a fact that my father sent them postcards every year until one too many came back unopened, or stayed afield unanswered. I let this slide, unsure whether her parents have lied to her or whether she was lying to me.

I ask her open-ended questions like a reporter. Maybe some of it has rubbed off. The questions must be good because they get me answers. My aunt Audrey tells me that Robin died from choking on food and that she's buried in Brooklyn. I look out my window, my corner of Brooklyn. I wonder how close my mother is to me right now. She tells me that Robin was in and out of mental institutions until she died. Her last psychiatrist worked on the Upper East Side. The edges of the world snap into focus. I don't indulge in my historical enemy—hope—but when she offers the shrink's name I jot it down. I'm still scribbling when she mentions my sister.

Her name is Mari, she says. She's thirty-five and lives in Maine. She never knew Robin either. After Robin had me she fled to Israel and worked for Teddy Kollek, the mayor of Jerusalem. She gave Mari up for adoption when she was an infant. My aunt doesn't say much more about Mari, except that she was severely abused by her adopted parents and has come out the worse for wear. The whimsical jaunt with me to Israel all of a sudden isn't so whimsical. Mari could have been me.

My heart and brain fall into a *Mikado* jumble. I try to pick out bloodied bits of resentment and hate, but all I feel is guilt. My sister didn't have a Ralph or a Mae or even a Jan. Racial confusion and some minor league poverty aside, I had it pretty good.

I have either a million questions or zero questions but I know nothing and too much for one day. My aunt says I have to make sure and visit her, her husband, and her two boys out in Miami immediately. All of a sudden I have a Jewish family with a big house with spare rooms on the beach. My American dream. I hang up, exhausted, and my phone rings immediately. It's my father, wondering where I am.

I overslept, I lied; *let's try for next week.*
No problem, my man. I'll be here.

Cool.

My aunt calls me a few days later and asks me if I've ever seen a picture of Robin. When I tell her I haven't, she says she'll try to find some to send me. She tells me a few more details about Robin and their side of the family. Robin was raised in Manhattan and attended the High School for the Performing Arts. She dropped in and out of college—Barnard, I think—but never finished. A brainy quitter—there was one point for nature over nurture. Did I know that my grandfather was one of the most influential Talmudic scholars of the twentieth century? All I know is that he is the same man who tried to talk my father into leaving my mother—I wouldn't have been born if it had been up to him. My aunt says that Robin and her father didn't get along. *Good for you, Mom*, I almost say, the word sticking like a peach pit in my throat. Robin had a *complicated* relationship with her parents, she says—there were no villains, just misunderstandings. I change the subject and ask her when she has in mind for my visit. She backs off with—*you know, we should take it slow—after all, I don't really know you.* A twinge of the hate I have fueled myself with for all these years rises to the surface like blood from the bone, and then evaporates.

CHAPTER XVII

HOME COME THE ANGELS

Miraculously, Dr. Harriet Harris was not only alive but still practicing in a tony high-rise apartment on the Upper East Side. *I'll be happy to talk to you about your mother,* she'd said when I called her. *You were raised in Israel, isn't that right?* A wave of guilty relief sluiced over me. *No, I'm her firstborn. Her son.*

———•———

A Hispanic doorman with the works—hat, tasseled epaulets—lets me in and points me to an elevator as big as my apartment.

Dr. Harris is just coming up on or has just said goodbye to seventy. She must have been fresh out of residency when she treated my motheer. She's tall—my height, maybe six feet—and reminds me of Lynn Redgrave.

We sit across from each other in designer chairs. The couch is off to my right. I wonder if my mother had lain there. Her office is frozen in mid-sixties design—Knoll and Eames pepper the space. It occurs to me that a week ago I barely knew my mother's last name.

So, exactly what do you want to know? I tell her the

thumbnail of my life but keep out the rough stuff. I tell her that I want to know anything she can tell me about my mother, good or bad. She asks me if I can handle it and I say yes. Cocking her silver head to the side, she tells me that Robin was a reactive schizophrenic and a severe bulimic on a heavy regimen of Thorazine and Haldol. She had OD'd many times, landing her in the hospital. According to Dr. Harris, Robin's father, Isaac, and her mother, Muriel, were both clinical paranoid schizophrenics. Her parents lived in Connecticut when Robin died, in a house with a room where Isaac went when he was "under the weather," to rave and gnash at the voices in his head. He was an imperious rabbi, a scrappy guy from New York's Lower East Side who married well, but always felt the sour breath of hot tenements at his heels.

Muriel Kahn was the daughter of a wealthy Minneapolis businessman. Her schizophrenia took the form of sociopathic remove: she was unable to form emotional ties with anyone, even her own daughter. While Isaac was controlling, Muriel disapproved of Robin's choices and let her know it. Robin spent her life trying to win the affection of a woman who was medically unable to feel empathy or give support. Dr. Harris says bulimia is a common by-product of a controlling parent. Isaac didn't help matters—but Robin could write him off as her antagonist. Fathers are supposed to be gruff and controlling.

Muriel's influence was more insidious. She wasn't domineering; she was *critical*. Because Robin's mother appeared to be the more "reasonable" parent, her put-downs went deep into Robin's psyche. Muriel dispassionately told Robin of the ways in which she (Robin) had failed her, and Robin took her mother at her word. Before Robin met my father, she had attempted suicide by taking a handful of sleeping pills, which Muriel used as a truncheon to prove to Robin how worthless she was. Food was the salve for Robin's ego. She would binge for hours after a confrontation with her mother. Raw meat was her favorite.

In 1972, just after Mari had been given up for adoption, Robin OD'd on her medication and was flown from Tel Aviv to Metropolitan Hospital in New York, where she was referred to Dr. Harris. For the next five years, Robin had sessions three to four times a week. Her parents gave her an allowance; her full-time job was therapy. After two abandoned kids and a lifetime of mental illness, Robin was determined to get better. Right after she started seeing Dr. Harris, the young doctor contracted pneumonia, putting a halt to their sessions for three weeks. Robin's bond with the doctor was so strong that she waited with no relapse and no substitute physician. *That kind of loyalty was impressive*, Dr. Harris said.

Robin never spoke of me, nor Mari. Dr. Harris knew of my existence but little more. Robin was never meant to have kids, the doctor said—she could barely take care of herself. She added that my mother was funny and smart, and that she liked to poke fun at herself.

A time line was starting to piece itself together. Robin tried to kill herself once—when she was in her early twenties—just before she met my dad. I could now remember my dad telling me that when he met Robin she was living in a halfway house. Dr. Harris said that first attempt was halfhearted, and had scared Robin away from trying it again. Her later ODs—there were a few— were all accidental, attempts at self-medication gone wrong. Robin took more of her medication to mute her anxiety, and was as surprised as anyone else when this would land her in the hospital. By 1977, Robin had gone five years without a single OD. And then, on the evening of Sunday, May 1, 1977, her mother called.

Robin was living in Brooklyn, working part-time as a bookkeeper, and almost ready, at thirty-eight, to be an independent woman. That Friday, her employer had asked her if she might like to work a few extra hours. Robin gratefully accepted. Starting bright and early the following Monday, she would begin working nearly full-time. Robin and her mother spoke once a week, every Sunday night. Robin excitedly told Muriel of her new schedule, to which her mother replied, *You know you're not as strong as normal people. Why would you try to be something you're not?*

Robin felt the old pressures return. She doubled her medication and pulled a plate of raw chuck from the fridge.

Robin tore the meat apart with her fingers and began

shoving the bloody strips into her mouth. A few minutes later, the medication kicked in. Thorazine and Haldol, even at double the recommended dosage, are not life-threatening. Their effects are calming; the greatest danger they pose is to dull the involuntary reflexes. Robin's muscles wouldn't work. She couldn't swallow. Alone in her Brooklyn apartment, choking, my mother panicked. She ran from the apartment in her nightgown, banging on doors down two flights of stairs until she collapsed at the front landing. She was dead before any of her neighbors had time to look through their peepholes.

Dr. Harris tells me she knows the details of my mother's last moments from the autopsy report. Jewish cemeteries do not admit suicides. I wonder if the Kahns were relieved to be told that Robin hadn't tried to kill herself. I also wonder if they found their psychological homicide preferable to her suicide. Dr. Harris tells me that Robin's sickness was a deadly match with that of her parents. She says she can't think of anything else, but do I have any questions.

At the door, when she says it seems like my father has done a great job, I realize that I haven't cried yet but if I don't leave right now I might. I thank her. She says, *Robin Matthews was one of my favorite patients.* I stop in the foyer and correct: *Kahn.* She looks at me, her head again at a gentle tilt: *Robin never changed her name—I knew her as Matthews and she died as a Matthews—it's on her headstone.* I press my hand into her flesh, shut the

door, and rock on my heels out in the hallway. I pray for
the elevator because I can't do this here. When it comes,
empty, the ride is not long enough.

As I walk the seventy blocks to my subway stop at
Union Square, I stop in Central Park and call my pop. I
need to tell him that he saved my life. That it was only
myself, not him or his skin, I had forsaken all those years
ago. I want to say to him what I guess he's always known,
that part of being a man is caring for your people or the
people who are yours and there may be a difference but I
can't tell right now. I tell him about Dr. Harris and about
the last three days, and when he hears how Robin died he
sighs long and hard into the phone, *Aw, no.* I ask if he had
loved her and he says he did. I ask him if he ever knew she
was ill. He says he didn't, that looking back and hearing
this, he caught her in a *lucid snapshot.* Only at the end did
he see the signs. I ask if he might have stayed with her
forever if it had stayed the way it was for them in the beginning. *Absolutely,* he says, then after a beat, *but it
didn't.* I stumble through a thank you but he stops me
and says, *I love you; you're my son.*

By the time I get home the sun is going scarlet, fighting to the last. There's a sheaf of mail in the vestibule,
which I take upstairs and toss on the table. I empty half
a gallon of water in long drafts. The return address on the
Fedex eight-by-ten envelope reads Miami. My aunt has
sent me pictures of my mother. I had imagined my
mother's face in dreams and in the negative space of my

own features for thirty-seven years. I study the pull tab at the top of the envelope like it's a combination lock. I pick at it. I need to have a moment of something before I see her for the first time.

I need to block from my mind the images left by Dr. Harris. I don't want to meet my mother among the dead. I remember my grandma as a living loving creature who cared for me so I tuck Robin into a thawing corner of my heart as a living loving creature, hurting too much to have stayed. I realize that many of the demons I have fought and mostly won were given to me by my mother. Maybe she had had to lose her battles so that I could win mine. I don't hate her. I won't look into her eyes, my eyes, and hate her. I never met her, not really, but I know that from this moment on, I will protect her memory from myself.

It's hard to swallow. I peel the tab from the envelope and force the lump past my throat. As the sun goes down in a fury of bruised purple and bloodied copper, I slide the photograph from the envelope. I am careful not to bend the edges.

ACKNOWLEDGMENTS

The author would like to thank the following, without whom neither the pages herein nor my life would have been possible: Ralph Dawson Matthews Jr.; Lauren Sandler; my editor, Vanessa Mobley; Kate Lee and Jon Huddle at ICM; Todd Sharp; and Stuart Adamson.

ABOUT THE AUTHOR

DAVID MATTHEWS is a writer living in New York.